Issues

in Justice

EXPLORING POLICY ISSUES
in the Criminal Justice System

EDITED WITH CONTRIBUTIONS BY

Roslyn Muraskin

 Wyndham Hall Press

ISSUES IN JUSTICE
Exploring Policy Issues in the Criminal Justice System

Edited with Contributions by

Roslyn Muraskin

Cover design by Melinda Dunithan

Library of Congress Catalog Card Number
90-050420

ISBN 1-55605-168-9 paperback
ISBN 1-55605-169-7 hardback

Dedicated to

My Husband Matthew

and our children

Seth, Craig & Tracy

TABLE OF CONTENTS

PREFACE

This book represents some critical issues we face in the criminal justice system with implications for policy changes. The authors address real issues and suggest real solutions. This work represents an attempt to increase our understanding of the problems faced by an already overburdened criminal justice system.

The field continues to change. New technology, new crimes impact on our system. The authors are well versed in their respective fields representing varied backgrounds. But each in his/her own way has something very important to contribute to the field. What is demonstrated in this work is the need to work within the system and to develop strategies in planning for the future. The twenty-first century is almost upon us and still we struggle to find the **justice** in criminal justice.

Roslyn Muraskin
Long Island University

CHAPTER ONE

INTRODUCTION

ISSUES IN JUSTICE: POLICY IMPLICATIONS

Roslyn Muraskin

There is no day that passes that we are not besieged with news of crime and its impact on society. We read about revolving door justice and the lack of the effectiveness of the criminal justice system. There are so many issues that pervade our justice system that oftentimes we find ourselves overwhelmed by what this system's true goals and objectives are. When criminologists, jurists, attorneys, educators find themselves disagreeing as to what the issues are and their possible solutions, we recognize we have a problem.

This book looks at some of the current issues that impact our criminal justice system, a system that calls out for decisions, for justice and for fair treatment. Crime affects our daily lives. How then do we decide what constitutes what is right and what constitutes what is wrong. The criminal justice system is an ever changing system and what needs to be decided are what determines our policies. Discussion focuses on some key issues, that is not to say this is a complete list but perhaps is a beginning.

What then are our policies? Who should make these policies? There are those critics of the system who indicate that policy is a result of emotion rather than based on solid research. This text has been developed to focus on issues faced within the criminal justice profession, such as corrections, ethical issues, victim rights, theories, alternatives to corrections, policing, probation and parole, the rights of children, and females. These writings represent a sampling of those areas where we have most concern.

As Wilson points out "crime is a pervasive problem that leaves few Americans untouched." During the past few decades two lessons have emerged: "crime was a far more intractable problem than we had earlier led to believe; and second, that there was clear room for improvement of deployment of resources to control crime" (Wilson, 1983: xi). This book aims not to present answers but rather to educate the student and professionals of what research has been done, where we should look for current strategies and tactics with suggestions being made to implement and develop policy.

Recidivism is a problem in today's criminal justice system. We incarcerate more inmates than ever before. Yet, most of these inmates will be released back into society. There are major policy implications to be decided. Welch's and Holzman's article focuses on policy issues, recommendations and training of inmates as they are involved with the "National Issues Forums Correction Project." The article's main thrust is in the arena of improving motivation, research, understanding and the training of inmates in the uses of periodical research information. How do we best deal with inmates and train them to succeed in the outside world.

Law enforcement agencies have many problems. One problem they are confronted with are hostage situations. What motives do hostage takers have, and what should be the response of police officers to such situations? What are the practical and ethical aspects of how the police should respond to hostage situations? Can police/should police lie or use deception when dealing with hostage takers is the thesis of an article by Grant Stitt. Psychological factors play a large role in hostage taking situations, thereby necessitating the construction of psychological profiles. In the end it is the goal of law enforcement to see to it that the hostages are not harmed. What policies, therefore, need to be developed to insure such safety?

As we deal with the criminal so too we must deal with victims. Certain standards of fair treatment must be afforded to victims as fair treatment is afforded to defendants. The criminal justice system as pointed out by Karmen is under continuous attack. There is either too much permissiveness or too many inequities. But what of the victim -- what rights does he/she have? Where is the justice system, when victims are ignored? The implementation of victim's rights poses a challenge to those involved with the criminal justice system. Dr. Karmen makes suggestions, that can impact on all those concerned with the victim and the system.

Gould and Sayles point out that "recent criminological theory has been shifting away from a focus on individual offenders to a focus on crime itself." Using such a focus, the authors point out that this shift might "provide a theoretical means for avoiding criminological and correctional arguments about human nature," and therefore review the implications for corrections. The authors suggest that an interactionist approach to crime might well shed some light on how corrections should be expected to fulfill their objectives.

Prisons are overcrowded and in most cases unable to rehabilitate the inmates. Alternative programs are on the rise nationwide. In looking at the goals and objectives of prisons, Reichel and Gauthier discuss a prison alternative, i.e. "boot camp corrections" or "shock incarceration." Its goal is to reduce overcrowding and/or recidivism. Their study indicates the support of the public particularly when helping the non-violent offender.

There exists a highly fragmented police force in this country. Nardini in his work advocates the consolidation of all police agencies. He is critical, for example, of the way sheriffs are chosen, citing supplication of services as well as resources, personnel, etc.. He recommends a reorganization of the police organization. There needs to be a more effective police organization in order to do the job. Nardini offers suggestions for change.

Implicit in policy change must be the teaching and practice of ethics in criminal justice. Ethics is not a term that belongs solely with the teaching of philosophy. In today's world, ethics or the lack of it play a role in the operation of criminal justice. The authors Schmidt and Victor offer suggestions of how ethics should be taught, its relevance in teaching and its importance in the practice of criminal justice.

Traditionally the probation officer and parole officer are appointed from civil service lists. Since 1972 such agencies have become unionized. What are the trends and how and what problems arise with its unionization are the topics of concern by Jamieson and Smith. What would happen if these personnel were to strike? The courts have supported the unionization of those in the public sector. The authors' findings indicate that such union activity does not hinder evaluation policies of new officers, but do impact on policies in other areas.

Those in criminal justice tend to label the good guys and the bad guys. Important, however, is the safeguarding of children from being labeled delinquent or pre-delinquent without substantial backup. Smith indicates the need for researchers to be careful in publishing results that have not been pretested. There needs to be the avoidance of labeling children who are what Smith refers to as defenseless. In determining delinquency, more care needs to be given to reaching conclusions before labeling young people bad guys.

Case studies are always useful in demonstrating the problems as they exist, or if problems exist; and, what recommendations to make or conclusions to reach. Such is the case with our last two articles. Traditionally, there has been much concern on how well a female could handle herself in what historically has been a man's job, i.e. a corrections officer. Rita Simon and Judith Simon studied a correctional facility in Michigan where the latter was employed and observed how well female correctional officers performed at an all male institution. Their article focuses on female roles in the criminal justice system. Implied in the authors' study is that females can do the same job as their male counterparts without regard to their sex. Gender makes no difference when it comes to working.

And lastly, Palmiotto and Padgett study how important is the use of patrol in police departments. How quickly are officers deployed? How efficient are these officers? Work productivity is important, when we study police and the criminal justice system. The authors using a case study in Savannah, Georgia comment on how productive patrol units are. They indicate the need to study the workload productivity of all police to get the most efficient deployment of patrol units. Implied is the more efficient the police are, the better able they will be able to perform making for a more efficient and effective system.

The lessons to be learned from these articles is that much needs to be done to improve our criminal justice system. There are no easy answers, but many questions. We recognize the goals of the system, but do not always agree on the means to the end. This text is to make you take notice of some areas of concern and realize "we've come a long way, but where are we going now?"

REFERENCE

Wilson, James Q. (1983). CRIME AND PUBLIC POLICY. San Francisco: Institute for Contemporary Studies.

CHAPTER TWO

THE NATIONAL ISSUES FORUMS CORRECTIONS PROJECT: AN INNOVATIVE APPROACH TO EXISTING NON-TRADITIONAL INMATE EDUCATION*

Michael Welch

and

Herbert Holzman

As prisons warehouse increasingly more inmates, social policy involving corrections has become fundamentally one-dimensional: that is, to build more prisons. In the midst of the debate over constructing more prisons, an important issue is often neglected by those advocating a "tough on crime" agenda. Policy "experts" often fail to recognize that one function of incarceration is to reduce recidivism. With recidivism rates alarmingly high, it is once again necessary to examine what is being done for inmates to prepare them for their return to the community. This paper explores this area of corrections in presenting an innovative approach to inmate education embodied in THE NATIONAL ISSUES FORUMS CORRECTIONS PROJECT. In addition to describing the development and operation of this new program and the inmate and institutional benefits derived, policy implications are also discussed.

---

*The views and opinions expressed in this article represent those of the authors and not those of the corrections officials who are mentioned. The authors thank the anonymous reviewers for their helpful comments and acknowledge Marie Mark for her assistance in preparing the final version of this article.

INTRODUCTION

The debate on corrections has resurrected the controversy concerning the role prisons should play in American society. While many politicians and lawmakers have concluded that a "war on crime" requires an arsenal of expanded and newly constructed prisons, there has been little discussion about what steps might be undertaken in prisons to reduce recidivism among inmates. Consequently, the current state of the correctional crisis is best understood as a contradiction: that is, contemporary correctional policy consists of massive incarceration while ignoring the obvious problem of recidivism. Despite the flaws inherent in this correctional policy, public opinion still favors massive incarceration over alternatives to imprisonment. Perhaps this paradox is better understood when the prison's raison d'etre is subject to critical examination. Shover and Einstadter contend that "the prison will always remain, not because imprisonment is a successful social practice, but because the prison symbolizes the anger generated by crime" (1988, p. 207).

It is clear that the public casts a cynical and skeptical eye on the ability of prisons to reform inmates. Ironically, though prisons are often believed to "not work," most citizens still favor the continued construction of additional prisons. This reinforces the accepted notion that the social function of prisons is not necessarily to reform criminals, but rather to simply impose punishment.

Although the debate over corrections has thus far concentrated on punishment and the construction of more prisons, this article addresses some difficult questions regarding correctional policy and inmate programs. For example, what types of educational programs should be offered to inmates that can better prepare them to return to the community? It is important to denote that inmates generally constitute a non-traditional group which, therefore, require educational programs that emphasize a non-traditional approach.

The scope and purpose of this article is to focus largely on the National Issues Forums Corrections Project, which is an innovative approach to existing non-traditional inmate education. In setting the stage for a broader discussion of the significance of all inmate programs, the current correctional crisis is briefly summarized.

THE CURRENT CORRECTIONAL CRISIS

By the end of June 1989, the number of state and federal inmates hit a national record totaling 673,565. Over the past eight years, the inmate population increased 90 percent and is currently expanding by about 800 prisoners a week (Bureau of Justice Statistics, 1989a). The immediate correctional crisis is further compounded by an increase in recidivism. A study by the Bureau of Justice Statistics (1989b) focused on 11 states and found that 63 percent of the inmates released were rearrested for a felony or serious misdemeanor within three years of discharge.

Due to massive incarceration, inmates in some correctional systems are likely to serve less time in order to make room for the newly incarcerated. Florida's state correctional system, for example, demonstrates how policy and practice can be self-defeating. The Florida prison system is so overcrowded that it is under court order to release a prisoner every time a new one is added (The New York Times, 1989). As suggested by these developments, correctional policy can no longer solely concern itself with the construction of prisons without recognizing the problems of recidivism. Subsequently, the nation is again faced with the difficult question of what should and could be done to prepare inmates for a successful return to the community.

In an effort to analyze the existing objectives of correctional policy, it is useful to identify the historical trends in corrections. Cohen (1985) demonstrates that corrections alternates between two mutually exclusive objectives: those of inclusion and exclusion. Inclusion, as understood in corrections, involves implementing measures which advocate integrating the offender into the community. Probation, parole, pre-trial diversion, and pre-release programs all fit into this category. At the other end of the continuum is exclusion, which emphasizes removing the offender from society.

Correctional policy in the 1960's is depicted as having utilized inclusionary measures, and as a result, numerous alternatives to incarceration surfaced during this time. The 1980's, however, were dominated by exclusion as evidenced by the vast number of incarcerations (Shover & Einstadter, 1988). This is a particularly disturbing trend considering that the overall crime rate dropped during this period. Meanwhile, the consensus of those in power continue to favor the building of more prisons, and the old adage "lock them up and throw away the key" has returned as a popular expression.

Although exclusionary measures currently exist as the prevailing practice in corrections, the fact that many inmates are frequently sent back to prison makes it incumbent upon policy-makers to reconsider the importance of preparing inmates to successfully return to the community. The major flaw of contemporary exclusion is best understood as a "correctional boomerang." The more society relies on massive incarceration to banish the criminal population, the more it can expect high rates of recidivism. Because incarceration serves only as "temporary" exclusion, inclusionary methods need to be incorporated into existing inmate programs. One approach in preparing inmates for their re-entry into society is the enrichment of the non-traditional educational programs in prisons.

THE NATIONAL ISSUES FORUMS

The History of the National Issues Forums

In 1981 the National Issues Forums were initiated by a nationwide network of not-for-profit organizations that combined to sponsor community forums. Sponsoring organizations included colleges, universities and schools; museums and historical associations; churches, synagogues and theological centers; community television stations; civic, labor, and professional organizations; student groups and senior citizen centers. The Kettering Foundation is one of several organizations that helped develop and expand these Forums to the extent that they are now being conducted in 48 states involving approximately 300,000 people.

The Forums may be seen as modern counterparts to the historical public dialogues of the Greek polis, and to the colonial American concept of the "Town Meeting." It is not the goal of the Forums to reach a consensus, or to support a specific point of view, or to advocate one single solution to the national issue under consideration. Rather the goal is to advance the individual views of the many, find the common thread that runs through these disparate views, and subsequently define the limits within which viable, broadly supported public policy may be built. This is the heart of the Forums, and they have indeed proven to be successful in fulfilling the goals and ambitions of their founders.

The Forums are conducted on the simple premise that in a democratic society, critical decisions should be made with public participation. In order to accomplish this most effectively, policy options need to be spelled out. And this is precisely what occurs in the Forums. Those participating have an opportunity to "work through" the pros and cons of the different policy choices presented. Consequently, the proposed solutions reflect the concerns and values of the participants, and they do so without relying on the terminology of experts and public leaders.

The topics for discussion are planned a year in advance by the Forums' current participants, at which time an issue book for each topic is prepared. The books fully describe each issue, and, three or four choices of action, including their pros and cons, are presented. The business of the participants in the Forums is to discuss thoroughly each issue and weigh the available options.

The National Issues Forums Corrections Project

Those involved in running the Forums nationally soon became aware that the participants attracted to them were -- as usually happens in such public education efforts -- most often white-collar, middle-class, socially-conscious, white, better-educated citizens. The Forums were, therefore, not adequately reaching those significant groups in society which are often left out of the political mainstream -- the poor, the elderly, the not-so-literate, the immigrant, and, of course, prisoners. As a result, this worthwhile program, already designed and in existence in society at large, and one that could have practical value if conducted in prisons, was not reaching that segment in need of being included.

There exists consensus among those in corrections work that many prisoners need to learn to communicate more effectively with others, improve their self-esteem, and to envision themselves as part of the community. The National Issues Forums Corrections Project sets out to refine communication skills, enhance self-esteem and reduce social isolation by including inmates in meaningful dialogue on important national issues.

Among its objectives, this program sets out to help inmates attain a higher degree of "civic literacy." Inmates who participate in the Forums enhance their personal motivation, learn how to use a library and research questions, and how to apply information from newspapers and magazine articles to the subject they are discussing.

These Forums are thus a "process" of development rather than merely an educational experience.

Pilot Projects

Pilot projects were initiated in different geographic regions. In 1986-1987 correctional centers in New Mexico, Indiana, Minnesota, Ohio, and Georgia were selected to participate in the NIF Corrections Project. Program formats varied, often reflecting the philosophy of the particular institution or the needs of the prisoner participants. For many inmates, the Forums were a new experience that marked the first time they had participated in a discussion of social issues. They presented their own views and listened to the ideas expressed by others, including those views with which they disagreed.

At the Westville Correctional Center in Indiana, administrators ranked the Forums as one of the school's most widely accepted and highly respected efforts in ten years of existence. Over two hundred inmates were involved, representing different educational levels (ABE, GED, pre-college, college, vocational). Additionally, the Forums were televised and featured on area cable television stations, giving communities throughout Northwest Indiana a positive point of view on the educational programs at the prison and their corresponding achievements.

In the Hennepin County Adult Correction Facility of Minnesota, under the direction of forum moderators, the Forums found the inmates became enthusiastically involved in the issue discussions. In one instance, prisoners were given an opportunity to express their ideas in the presence of a District Attorney and a State Senator who were attending the session. The Forums thereby created an opportunity for a policy-maker to share ideas and gather information from men who are typically excluded from the mainstream of society.

At the Montgomery Correctional Facility in Mount Vernon, Georgia, prisoner participants also took part in the Forums with enthusiasm and interest. There were lively discussions, yet participants carefully listened to each other, and discussion moderators were impressed with the serious tone of the participants. Generating information in the context of group involvement was interpreted as a way for prisoners to build their citizenship skills.

In New Mexico, the Forums were conducted in four facilities. A State Director of Education, Cecil J. Smith, commented: "What most prisoners need is to improve their ability to get along with others. They need to learn to communicate, they need more people skills." The Forums offer such an opportunity and more. For example, one of the successes attributed to the Forums (and certainly one of its most significant goals) is that of a new curriculum which is now being offered in the four aforementioned prisons. Included in this curriculum are classes in the humanities, career awareness, life planning, and future studies -- all of them stressing communication.

Conducting the Forums in New York State

After the initial success of these pilots, it became important to test the program consistently and carefully in a number of comparable facilities in one jurisdiction. New York was selected for this demonstration project because of its size and the challenge it presented. Success in New York State could identify it as a flagship representative of an established national program.

In September 1987, Marion Borum, Deputy Commissioner of Program Services for New York State, took part in detailed discussions with the idea of introducing the Forums in New York State prisons. Impressed by the program, Commissioner Borum saw that the Forums fit well with other programs which had recently been inaugurated in the state. He recommended five facilities in which to launch the Forums: Green Haven (maximum security), Wallkill, Hudson and Arthur Kill (medium security), and Bayview (a women's facility). These institutions represented a cross-section of the inmate population.

In a memorandum to the five facilities' superintendents, Commissioner Borum wrote, "I have personally met with representatives of the sponsoring organization [The Kettering Foundation], and am convinced that they provide an educational experience that would be beneficial to inmates at your facility. Taking into account the fact that a substantial majority of our inmates enter prisons with very limited educational and cultural exposure, I believe that we can and should expand our efforts to help them in this regard. The evidence is that these forums successfully encourage and require inmate participants to be introspective as well as analytical so that they develop the ability to see beyond their own immediate, narrow, personal interests." Administrators in each of the five facilities agreed to engage in the Forums program.

The Forums were then expanded to include more prisons, and to date, Forums have been conducted in 11 New York facilities, five of which are maximum security. Certificates of Participation were presented to 296 inmates in 1988. Furthermore, the number of institutions and the number of inmates participating is expected to increase in the next few years.

How the Forums are Conducted

The key word in describing the Forums is "flexibility." As a result, no two Forums are exactly alike. For example, the number of inmates in each Forum (also referred to as study circles or discussion groups) varies, as does the number of meetings per week, the amount of time per meeting, and the place of meeting. However, the following format can be used as a general model: There are usually 10 to 15 inmates in a group which meets once a week for approximately an hour to an hour and a half. One topic remains the central focus of the group for six to eight meetings. At the conclusion of these meetings, a Final Forum is held at which all the inmates who have participated in the separate groups assemble together. It is here that the ideas, choices and solutions which have been raised at the individual meetings are openly expressed among all the participants.

The reading material for each topic is contained in issue books which are written and researched by the Public Agenda Foundation for Kettering. The books provide a source of information about the topic and serve as an excellent reference. Written at the fourth grade reading level, these books are easily mastered by the majority of inmates, and the material is carefully presented in a straight-forward, nonideological, nonpartisan manner. The inmates are also encouraged to do further reading in periodicals and newspapers on the topic. Inmates are asked to pay the $2.00 cost of the books. This is the only expense to anyone in the entire program. In some cases the cost of the books is paid for by the institution -- in whole or in part. However, inmates are encouraged to pay for the books themselves as they then have a vested interest in the program and have made a commitment of some kind.

The Moderators

A moderator is present at all discussion meetings, and can be any state correctional employee working in that prison. Some prison employees believe that there is no place in the prison for free speech, or for protecting the rights of others. They are often cynical or burned out and just go through the motions of performing their work. But others who decide, on their own, to become moderators do so because they are highly motivated. These employees have come to realize the importance of the forums in helping to maintain custodial stability, as well as providing educational benefits to the inmates. These moderators represent almost every type of prison staff: Teachers, counselors, therapists, secretaries, correction officers, chaplains, network administrators.

A one-day training session is held for potential moderators. In this seminar, the techniques, aims and procedures are reviewed. It is of importance to point out that the key to successful Forums are the moderators -- they represent the heart of the program. Theirs is the challenging task of being actively involved in the dialogue of the group, while remaining nonpartisan and impartial during the discussion. Further, it is essential that the moderator establish a cordial atmosphere so that ideas may be interchanged without the participants fearing rejection or personal humiliation.

Thus, the moderator should maintain a willingness to listen as well as have the skills to facilitate meaningful interaction. Moreover, the effective use of humor is a useful technique to transcend tense situations, and can assist in encouraging the participants to "work through" the issues.

The Final Forum

The Final Forum is the culmination of all the work and effort by everyone involved. It symbolizes a graduation - a rite of passage.

Upon completion of the material in the issue book by the various discussion groups, they then select representatives to speak on their behalf at the Final Forum. These representatives become a panel, and all the other inmates who have participated in the Forums are assembled as the audience. Inmates who have not participated are also invited. The Final Forum thus serves as a remarkable "selling tool" as the non-participating inmates get an opportunity to observe first hand just how worthwhile the Forums are.

In addition to the panel of inmates who have been selected to present the various positions and solutions on the topic, local VIP's are also invited to attend. In one particular maximum security facility, for example, a local Judge and a District Attorney were invited. They addressed the audience and then later answered questions put forth by the inmates. The topic for this session was "Crime," and the inmates appreciated having had the opportunity to listen to the guests, as well as express their own ideas on this vital subject.

Local television stations and newspaper reporters are also invited to the Final Forum. Through the media, the community at large can see and hear inmates intelligently discuss a major issue of the day. This helps breakdown the social stereotyping which often portrays prisoners as "animals." At the same time, it also provides inmates with a feeling of having been heard and seen in a positive light, something they do not often experience.

PRACTICAL SIGNIFICANCE & POLICY IMPLICATIONS

While correctional facilities that offer the Forums have found them useful to both inmates as well as staff, the institution itself can also benefit. For example, the Forums can facilitate the achievement of their organizational and social goals within the prison. In this light, the Forums are functional to the institution insofar as they improve inmate-staff relations which helps reduce the social distance between these groups. Additionally, the Forums can assist in maintaining custodial security by easing institutional conflict that sometimes sparks violence. Other organizational benefits include enhancing professionalism and improving staff morale among those who serve as moderators. This type of staff development also reduces staff cynicism and retreatism.

It should be noted that the Forums can become a viable inmate program without straining the institution's budget because the moderators are drawn from the existing pool of prison employees. However, administrators need to be cautious at the planning stages to avoid "horizontal loading" among the moderators. That is, if staff members volunteer as moderators, their supervisors need to be careful that these staff members have not taken on too many responsibilities. The balancing of institutional assignments requires informed managerial decision-making. Providing administrative attention is important so that the Forums, as well as other functions of the prison, are not inadvertently neglected or sabotaged. In sum, the Forums offer practical significance to the institution by engaging inmates and staff in meaningful interaction, as well as being beneficial to the internal order of the prison.

By identifying the practical significance of the Forums, these programs are likely to be considered suitable for future policy considerations. Thus, as correctional administrators recognize the utility of the Forums, the inmates themselves can see that the institution also values the importance of the program. The Forums have significant social relevance because they represent an institutional effort to prepare inmates for their release.

CONCLUSIONS

The Forums provide both short and long term benefits for inmates. As an immediate reward, the inmates gain information on a subject of vital importance to society. The long term gain is developed through the process itself -- by learning to think in terms of actions and consequences. This is particularly important for inmates who are generally prone to thinking and acting impulsively.

The Forums are also vehicles by which democratic principles can be introduced within the prison community. They are favorably viewed by the institutional staff, even among those employees who are only peripherally involved. Staff and administrators consider the Forums as providing valuable learning tools for the inmates, and equally important, they contribute to the prison's custodial stability.

The harsh reality of correctional policy today is that the current trend in corrections is dominated by exclusionary policies such as massive incarceration. Among the flaws inherent in exclusionary measures is that they do not adequately deal with recidivism. Consequently, there exists the need for more inclusionary measures in corrections, not merely because they are more humane but because they provide sensible alternatives to massive warehousing.

REFERENCES

Bureau of Justice Statistics (1989a). "Prisoners in 1988." **Bureau of Justice Statistics Bulletin.** Washington, D.C.: U.S. Department of Justice.

Bureau of Justice Statistics (1989b). "Recidivism of Prisoners Released in 1983." **Bureau of Justice Statistics Special Report.** Washington, D.C.: U.S. Department of Justice.

Cohen, Stanley (1985). **Visions of Social Control.** Cambridge, U.K.: Polity Press.

Shover, Neal, & Werner J. Eistadter (1988). **Analyzing American Corrections.** Belmont, CA: Wadsworth Publishing Company.

The New York Times. "Florida's Jammed Prisons: More In Means More Out." By Andrew H. Malcolm, July 3, 1989. Pp. A-1 and 9.

CHAPTER THREE

ETHICAL AND PRACTICAL ASPECTS OF POLICE RESPONSE TO HOSTAGE SITUATIONS*

B. Grant Stitt

This paper simultaneously analyzes the ethical and practical aspects of hostage situations confronted by law enforcement agencies. Discussion focuses on the likely motives of hostage taker(s) and police strategies most likely to result in the most moral end to the particular incident. Special attention is given to the need for police to lie or deceive hostage takers in certain situations in order to obtain the least harmful outcome. Also discussed is the relevance that the psychological state of the hostage taker(s) can have on the moral acceptability of the police strategy for dealing with the situation.

INTRODUCTION

Of all the situations confronted by police, few are as emotionally charged or psychologically complex as incidents in which hostages have been taken. The hostages are being used as pawns in a game that can prove deadly to many of the participants. The barricade-and-hostage scenario presents a no-win situation in which police strategies, procedures and competence will be highly scrutinized by sensationalist media coverage. Since the dynamics of hostage situations may vary along a number of different dimensions, it is necessary to analyze both practical and ethical consider-

*(The author wishes to thank Officer Donald Rutherford and Capt. Walter Crews of the Memphis Police Department, and Guy Meeks, Chief of Police, Mesa, Arizona for the technical assistance they provided.)

ations simultaneously. Of special concern is whether various strategies and procedures can be practical as well as ethical.[1]

It is necessary to first of all provide a definition of hostage situations. Next the various types of hostage situations will be delineated. Then, the logically possible response strategies that police could employ in hostage situations are delineated and evaluated. Special attention is given to whether or not it is morally acceptable for police to lie or use deception in dealing with hostage takers. Next, the psychological process of transference, commonly referred to as the Stockholm Syndrome,[2] and its advantages and disadvantages, as well as the ethical implications of police attempts to foster its development are discussed. Finally, the relationship between politics and hostage negotiations as well as the decision to assault are examined from an ethical point of view.

The Hostage Situation

A hostage situation exists when one or more persons seize another person or persons by force and hold them captive against their will for the purpose of bargaining to have certain demands met by authorities. Captives may be taken for the purpose of gaining attention or striking terror, but these captives are not hostages until such time as their value in a bargaining situation is realized by the captors. Barricaded situations are similar to hostage situations, but captives are generally absent and the perpetrator(s) may not have demands (i.e. some suicidal mental cases). Both types of situations are usually contained in one location. In either instance it is the desire of the police to contain the situation so as to prevent harm from coming to others outside of the police perimeter. Also, since the position of the police is strengthened if their control of the situation is maximized, and it is easier to strike a bargain from a position of strength, it is imperative that the police not allow the situation to become mobile. This is more important in the hostage situation than in the barricaded situation since the hostage taker(s) is already in a position of strength by having control over the life of the hostage or hostages. Nonetheless, if the person in the barricaded situation were to become mobile, they could possibly take hostages to strengthen their position and to keep the police at bay.

The police are more likely to be involved in an actual negotiation process with the hostage taker than with the barricaded individual because the lives of innocent people are at stake. Since the hostage situation has the potential to be highly volatile, the police must approach such situations with extreme sensitivity and caution. All things being equal, the hostage taker is more likely than the barricaded individual to possess a personality or belief system which is prone to violence. This is evidenced by the fact that he has taken innocent people captive and put them in a position of great danger.

Types of Hostage Takers

The Federal Bureau of Investigation and most domestic police departments divide hostage takers into four distinct categories. These categories are: (1) traditional (or criminal trapped at the scene of a crime or in the process of escaping from the scene of a crime), (2) terrorists, (3) prisoners and (4) the mentally disturbed (IACP (1975:2).

The traditional or criminal type often takes hostages to gain leverage in order to bargain for their freedom. It is important that the police initially determine if the criminal in this situation has a relatively "normal" personality, in which case he can be dealt with on a reality-oriented basis. If the criminal has a history of mental problems or is exhibiting symptoms of being mentally disturbed, then different negotiation strategies would need to be employed. Also, such an individual's mental capacity and personality characteristics must be continuously monitored and evaluated.

Of the four types of hostage takers, terrorists are probably the most dangerous (Beall, 1976:34). When terrorists take hostages, the operation is usually well-planned and extremely well-organized. Terrorists are so potentially dangerous because it is likely that they are prepared to die for their cause and it is also likely that they have no qualms about killing their hostages (Mickolus, 1976:1315). They are sophisticated fighters and it is probable that they have studied police anti-terrorist strategies and know exactly what to expect from police. Law enforcement officers, on the other hand, must convince the terrorists that killing hostages would severely discredit them no matter how valid their demands might be (Fuselier, 1981:5). If this can be accomplished, the situation might be successfully resolved since terrorists are very concerned about publicity and support for their cause. Fortunately, the United States has seen few terrorist acts within its boundaries. This is probably because the freedoms of speech and assembly allow groups to march and demonstrate and get publicity without having to resort to violent means.

The third type of hostage situation involves prisoners in jails or prisons who take hostages, usually correctional personnel, in order to gain leverage and get publicity for what they see as legitimate grievances concerning the conditions of their own captivity. Police response to attempts to take over a prison or jail is different from other hostage situations. Generally, the rule is to stall for time in order to obtain psychological profiles of the hostage takers, access the level of threat involved and hope the Stockholm Syndrome (discussed in depth later) takes effect. However, in what is usually a relatively unorganized riot situation, waiting may only allow for the emergence of true leaders and the organization of the whole prison population (Fuselier, 1981:5). Usually only a handful of inmates are aware of any plans for such an uprising to occur. Thus, in this type of situation the authorities should try to isolate the hostage-taking prisoners, along with the hostages, from the rest of the inmate population. Further, as with the terrorists, the police should try to convince those holding the hostages that no matter how valid their complaints may be, their cause will be severely discredited if they harm any of the hostages.

The final type of hostage taker is the mentally disturbed person. This type is the most prevalent and perhaps least dangerous, if properly trained personnel are dealing with them. With regard to mentally disturbed hostage takers, it is extremely important to construct personality profiles of the hostage takers and closely monitor any changes in mood or affect which may occur. For the sake of convenience four broad personality categories which make, clinically speaking, rather gross distinctions, are employed for diagnosis. These categories are: (1) paranoid schizophrenic, (2) manic-depressive (depressed type), (3) inadequate personality and (4) antisocial personality (Fuselier, 1981:3). These categories are by no means exhaustive or mutually exclusive. Often there may be co-mingling of characteristics of the various types. However, for the law enforcement officer, who is not a clinical psychologist or psychiatrist, these categories are sufficiently distinct and suggest the necessarily different negotiation strategies to successfully deal with very different types of personalities.

The paranoid schizophrenic is characterized by hallucinations often accompanied by feelings of persecution, delusions (fixed false beliefs which have no basis in reality), behavior consistent with the delusions (extreme anxiety and suspiciousness), and this type of individual is often hostile and aggressive (Fuselier, 1981:3). This type of person is frequently excessively religious. Since this person is quite out of touch with reality, it is important to realize that though this person is being told one thing he may be interpreting it to mean something entirely different. In negotiations with such individuals it is important not to dismiss the delusions, but instead to show interest in the delusions, without participating in them.

The manic-depressive hostage taker is virtually always in the depressed state when he takes hostages. The hostages are likely to be either family members or individuals known to the hostage taker. If their depression is extreme, persons of this type are likely to kill themselves and/or their hostages (Fuselier, 1981:4). The manic-depressive has very definite delusions about society and mankind and rationalizes the killing of his hostages by thinking that he is doing them a favor by removing them from an evil world. Besides being depressed, such individuals are likely to be uneasy, apprehensive, agitated and perplexed. Extreme guilt is another common characteristic exemplified in the depressed state. When in the depths of depression, an abrupt change in mood, signified by the hostage taker saying that "everything is okay now," may indicate that the individual has decided to kill the hostages and/or himself (Fuselier, 1981:4). For this reason a more gradual improvement in their mood is a better sign and the desired goal of negotiations.

The hostage taker who possesses an inadequate personality perceives himself to be a failure (Fuselier, 1981:4). He defines himself as a loser, is likely to have a poor employment history and be a member of the lower class. The taking of hostages may be an attempt to show people that he is important and can do something right. Because the individual with an inadequate personality is in touch with reality the police can usually establish meaningful dialogue. He is likely to be intelligent, but impractical and frequently changes his demands. Frequently, this type of individual is married to a domineering woman and has sexual irregularities (i.e., homosexuality, bisexuality, impotence). It is important not to allow friends or family to negotiate with this individual because this may reinforce his bad feelings about himself.

The last type of mentally disturbed hostage taker is the anti-social personality, also known as the sociopath or psychopath. He is usually identified as the "con man" and is quite adept at manipulating people (Fuselier, 1981:4). The antisocial personality is extremely dangerous because he is incapable of loyalty to groups, individuals, or social values. This person is grossly selfish, callous, irresponsible, impulsive and unable to feel guilt. He has a low tolerance for frustration, tends to be extroverted, is an adept liar and tends to blame others for his problems or provides plausible explanations for his behavior which seem to absolve him of responsibility. Because he is such a good "con man" he is difficult to deceive. Since he is easily bored and requires constant stimulation, it is important that the police constantly keep him thinking so that he does not turn on the hostages for a source of excitement (Fuselier, 1981:4). Fortunately, since individuals possessing an antisocial personality are usually not suicidal, it is possible to convince them that it is to their advantage to give up the hostages and surrender.

As should be apparent from this discussion of the different personality characteristics of the four categories of mentally disturbed hostage takers, it is crucial that police begin immediately to construct psychological profiles of the perpetrator(s). Such profiles can be the keys that will open the door to successful resolution of the hostage situations. Not enough emphasis can be placed on the value of closely monitoring hostage takers' mood swings and other symptoms of personality disorders because this can be used to determine when the situation is sufficiently dangerous to justify immediate intervention in the form of a tactical assault by police.

Response Strategies to Hostage Situations

It is generally agreed that there are five distinct strategies which the police employ in response to true hostage situations. The five strategies are: (1) attack or assault without making any attempt to negotiate; (2) neither negotiate nor assault, but attempt to wait out the hostage takers in the hope that time will result in peaceful resolution; (3) negotiate, but do not make concessions to demands; (4) negotiate and give in to demands; and (5) negotiate and lie about giving in to demands (Betz, 1982:110-111). In his critique of the morality of these response strategies Betz suggests that "...it is better to negotiate than to attack, better to negotiate honestly than dishonestly, and better to make small concessions to the hostage takers' demands than to adopt a policy of no concessions" (1982:111). However, the analysis that Betz provides is rather superficial. Unfortunately, the real world of hostage negotiating is quite different than he would have us believe. For example as Fuselier (1981) points out, FBI statistics indicate approximately 52% of all hostage situations involve hostage takers who fall into the "mental case" or "mentally disturbed" category. Betz, however assumes that more often than not hostage takers are rational and calculating terrorists.[3]

The only clear-cut advantage of an assault without attempting to negotiate strategy is that further hostage situations may be averted because of the deterrence factor. This outcome might only occur for a minority of the hostage situations, the prison and traditional (criminal) types of situations. It is unlikely that the persons suffering from mental disorders would be deterred, since their impairments of reason are assumed to render them undeterrable. A more important argument against this strategy is the fact that assaults tend to result in a high probability of casualties to hostages. A Rand Corp. study revealed that 78% of hostages were killed when an assault took place (Manning, 1985:30). Betz sums up the immorality of this strategy when he says, "There is something unintelligent, brutal, and inhumane in automatically deciding to attack hostage takers who are seeking to talk about their demands" (1982:113).

The second strategy, which is to neither negotiate nor attack, but wait the hostage taker(s) out, has two obvious advantages. First, the police would not be lying or deceitful about their intentions. Second, a waiting strategy may tend to facilitate the occurrence of the Stockholm Syndrome which in the long-run could be beneficial to the achievement of the harmless resolution of the entire situation. Regarding the development of the Stockholm Syndrome there seems to be significant documentation that it can be facilitated by police manipulation of interactions between the hostage taker(s) and the hostage(s) (Olin and Born, 1983). Such manipulations can only occur through police suggestions which require at least minimal dialogue between either the police and the hostage taker(s) or the police and the hostage(s). Suggestions can be made as police negotiate for minimal concessions.

Some situations, by their very nature, cannot be resolved by either waiting or standing mute. Examples are prison situations where quick resolution may prevent the amorphous rebels from becoming organized, or situations where the hostage takers are mental cases who must either receive stimulation (e.g., the antisocial personality, who without meaningful dialogue with the police may resort to brutalizing or killing his hostages) or need their ego built up and need to feel they have someone to depend on (e.g., depressed persons). A strict waiting strategy in such situations could result in disastrous outcomes.

In the final analysis there may be no such thing as a "no negotiation" strategy, since, as Betz (1982) points out, at a minimum the police would have to negotiate the terms of surrender. Thus, though this seems on its face to be an alternative, it would be neither practical nor really possible for the police to say nothing.

The third strategy, negotiate without concessions, can certainly be used to buy time. The use of this strategy, implies at least the use of minor concessions or compromises. In other words, there must be some good-faith attempts at compromise. It is certainly possible to have meaningful dialogue without giving in to the major demands of the hostage takers. Further, small concessions may foster the development of trust which may result in surrender and peaceful resolution of the situation. This is especially true where the hostage taker is mentally disturbed.

The fourth strategy, negotiation with concessions, is not acceptable if the concessions made are major ones. As Betz states, "The objection to capitulating to such demands is that it rewards evil, gives in to blackmail, and encourages those who would perform similar actions in the future" (1982:117). It is of paramount importance that hostage takers not be allowed to be successful in realizing their demands, especially for the purpose of deterring future hostage situations. Giving in to minor situational demands (i.e., requests for food, cigarettes, or other comforts) should not be confused with major types of demands such as transportation, exchange of hostages, or freedom. Regarding such minor concessions Betz says:

> To negotiate with hostage takers, capitulating partially (if partial capitulation means meeting demands that should be met anyway or making harmless promises about future behavior) in order to gain the release of the hostages and the surrender of their captors is to negotiate successfully. No one is wronged, no more persons are hurt than were hurt before the successful negotiations. The terrorist is arrested and jailed, and the future of the attempt stands as a deterrent to future hostage takers (1982:118-119).

Generally speaking, the history of hostage negotiating in the United States reflects the repeated success of the police in resolving hostage situations without harm to hostages, hostage takers or police personnel [see, for example Bolz and Hershey (1979)] through the use of negotiating techniques. None of the hostage situations handled by major law enforcement agencies have included concessions of major proportions.

The fifth strategy, to negotiate and lie about giving in to demands, is certainly not condoned as a general approach to hostage situations. In fact, in both policy and procedure for hostage situations, the authorities do not set out to lie to the perpetrators. The principle that they follow is to set up meaningful dialogue with the perpetrators so that concessions can be made which are acceptable to both sides. This is contrary to what Betz (1982) seems to suggest, which is that the police set out to engage in a lying match with the hostage taker(s). This is not the case. Deceit is used at times but only when necessary. Whether or not the police need to use deception must be discussed in a broader sense.

The Use of Deception

Is it ever necessary for the police to lie or use other types of deception in the process of negotiating with a hostage taker?[4] The position that is taken here is that it may often be necessary for some form of deception to be used in order to achieve the most desirable end to a hostage situation. The use of deception in such a situation results in what Klockars (1980) referred to as "the Dirty Harry problem," which is a genuine moral dilemma in law enforcement. Klockars defines such a dilemma as a situation in which the "ends to be achieved are urgent and unquestionably good and only a dirty means will work to achieve them" (1980:33). Klockars further specifies that such a dilemma is one from which "one cannot emerge innocent no matter what one does -- employ a dirty means, employ an insufficiently dirty means or walk away" (1980:22). It is, however, quite unlikely that police officers involved in hostage negotiations would perceive their use of deception as in any way immoral or ethically unacceptable, due to the very nature of the hostage situation.

The use of deception by police officers in the hostage situation meets Klockars' criteria for a type or Dirty Harry problem: the goal is unquestionably good in that police are attempting to save lives and the situation is clearly urgent. What remains is to determine whether or not the use of deception constitutes "dirty means". Deception is the act of causing someone to accept as true or valid something that is in fact false or invalid. Though deception may not be a verbal act, such misrepresentation is engaged in for the purpose of intentionally misrepresenting or falsifying some form of information, such as disguising a police officer as a pilot who will supposedly fly the hostage takers to their desired destination.

Since the use of deception represents the conveying to another of an untruth, the conveying of such an untruth may be dirty means if the person is entitled to the truth. It should be clear that by virtue of his actions, the commandeering of innocent people and the threatening of lives, the hostage taker does not qualify as one who has a **right** to the truth. As Betz points out, he should not expect to hear the truth.

> ...surely the aggressor does not expect to be told the truth in such situations. A coerced promise is no promise. One can compel others to speak when holding a gun on them, but the bully can only expect to hear what he or she wants to hear, not the truth. Just as no member of a liar's club expects to hear the truth, so no hostage taker should expect to hear the truth in the sort of situation that he or she creates. (Betz, 1982:122)

Nonetheless, just because the hostage taker neither has a right to the truth, nor may expect to hear the truth, this should not entitle the police to deceive hostage takers whenever they desire.[5] Ideally, before the police use deception, they should know that this act will result in the achievement of the desired end of minimizing harm to all involved. Unfortunately, this probably can not be known with a great deal of certainty. The ultimate utility of any action taken by the police in a hostage situation will not be known until the situation is resolved. At the moment of the decision about whether or not to deceive the hostage taker the estimation of the ultimate utility of such action is at best a probability assessment. This assessment is made on the basis of outcomes of previous similar hostage situations and the extent of the intelligence material compiled on the motives and personality characteristics of the present hostage taker(s).

Assuming the use of deception to be dirty means, Klockars (1980) argues that three criteria must be met in order to justify the use of dirty means. First, it must be possible that the dirty means could result in the desired ends. Second, there are no means other than dirty means which could result in the desired ends. Finally, if the dirty means are the only ones available, in the end it is believed they will not be in vain.

In many hostage situations peaceful resolution could result from the use of deception. The other two criteria may remain doubtful at the time that the decision about the use of deception must be made. First of all, with regard to whether deception is the only means which could result in desired ends, it is obvious that telling the complete truth (i.e. that the T.A.C.T. squad is about to assault, or to tell a mental case with an inadequate personality that they are a failure and that this episode is simply another example of their messed-up life) would often be disastrous. At the same time deceptions that might easily be detected or that are simply unnecessary are foolish and could harm police credibility in the community and in other hostage situations. In the final analysis the end may justify the means only if it is the only means available. As Bok notes, "Even if a lie saves a life, it is unwarranted if the liar was aware that a truthful statement could have done the same" (1979:93).

The effect of whatever means are chosen will be known only after the situation has been resolved. Due to the volatile and emotionally charged nature of hostage situations the best decisions which can be made are informed decisions, where both quantity and quality of information are important. Situations can change rapidly, especially if the police do not have control of the immediate environment. Therefore, hostage situations require highly trained personnel who can cope with such situations and who can rely on previous experiences of their own and other law enforcement agencies with similar situations.

The long term advantages or disadvantages of strategies that include deception are by no means clear. As Betz points out, "...if the police or other negotiators tell the truth in every instance of negotiating, it will have the best effect in the long run (1982:122)." The reason for this is that if the police deception is discovered during the negotiation process and this becomes generally known, their credibility will be harmed, making subsequent negotiation attempts more difficult and increasing the likelihood that they will fail. It is also possible that if the police consistently tell the truth and do not attempt to deceive the hostage taker, their high level of credibility in negotiating may result in potential hostage takers believing that they can profit from the negotiation situation resulting in an increase in the frequency of hostage taking. This assumes that the potential hostage taker is rational and carefully analyzes the possible outcomes of his or her actions. It seems likely that only those potential hostage takers who think rationally will be affected by police deception. Thus, if the police use deception when the use of such techniques seems justified to maximize control over a situation and where not using such methods might jeopardize the well being of the hostages, hostage taker or police personnel, deterrence may be achieved. Deterrence would be achieved because the rationally thinking potential hostage taker will likely reason that the outcome of the situation will be that his demands will not be met due to police trickery and/or he may be killed in the process. Thus the use of deception may act as a deterrent to those who are deterrable. However, since many hostage takers are mentally disturbed, the deterrent effect of police deception may be minimal. It must be reiterated that the use of such techniques should not be indiscriminate. The hostage taker could become enraged and violent upon realizing that the police have lied or utilized other forms of deception.

The Stockholm Syndrome

The Stockholm Syndrome is the popular term for the process of transference, which commonly develops in hostage situations. There are three elements of this phenomenon (Olin and Born, 1983:20):

(1) Positive "feelings" from the hostages to their captor(s);

(2) Negative "feelings" toward authorities by both hostages and captor(s); and

(3) Positive "feelings" returned by the captors to the hostages

The onset of these symptoms is believed to be a function of the relationship between the hostage taker and hostages, the length of time of captivity, and the physical as well as social distance between the hostage taker and hostages. Further, the development of this transference process is dependent on the nature of the interaction between the hostage taker and the hostages. As Miller states, "If the interaction is hostile, transference will generally not take place" (1980:43). The transference is actually a change of identity in which it seems that the hostages, due to their captivity and total dependence on the hostage takers, develop a dependency relationship with the hostage taker. Then the hostages begin to empathize with the hostage taker's motives or cause and actually come to redefine the relevant issues in ways similar to those of their captors. As this process continues, they also redefine the position of the police relative to the total situation and come to view them as enemies or at best, antagonists. This change on the part of the hostages is viewed positively by the hostage takers and acts to reduce the social distance between themselves and the hostages. This third stage of the trans- ference process is actively sought by authorities because the more positive the feelings that the hostage takers have toward hostages, the less likely it is that they will harm them.

There are factors which can preclude the occurrence trans- ference. For example, generally transference will not occur if there are established racial or ethnic hostilities between the hostage taker and hostages. Such hostilities create such great social distance that no practical amount of interaction or common experience can overcome their effects. Also, transference will be precluded when "the hostage is capable of maintaining some intellectual distance, which enables the objective assessment of one's plight as having been wrought by one's captors" (Miller, 1980:44). Some sophisticated hostage takers, mostly terrorists, have deliberately structured their hostage situations to minimize the occurrence of such transference. Realizing the possibility that they will have to kill all or some of their hostages, they have attempted to inhibit the development of interpersonal relationships by segregating hostages or blindfolding or gagging them. Such methods have been employed by the South Moluccans in the Netherlands and by the Japanese Red Army (Olin and Born, 1983:22). It also should be pointed out that the personality of the hostage taker may preclude the entire transference process from occurring. The person with an antisocial personality can use his superficial charm and superior intelligence to "con" the hostages to empathize with him and may get their support. On the other hand, his inability to establish sincere emotional relationships would prevent him from entering the third phase to the transference process in which he might be genuinely concerned for the welfare of the hostages (Lanceley, 1981:32).

Though there are benefits of the Stockholm Syndrome, there are also disadvantages. As Miller points out, negotiators must learn that it is necessary to be leery of trusting hostages. "Hostages can easily become unwitting accomplices of their captors, especially when transference takes place to the extent that hostages perceive police and not their captors as being the primary obstacle to freedom," says Miller (1980:45). For example, during her captivity in the mid 1970's, newspaper heiress Patty Hearst, after undergoing what appears to have been a total instance of transference, provided covering gunfire as her captor-accomplices escaped a bungled shoplifting attempt.

Fuselier (1981) summarizes what he sees as the negative aspects of the possible development of the Stockholm Syndrome. First of all, the transference of identity phenomena

may result in a situation in which any or all of the information coming to the police through the hostages may be
unreliable.[6] Also, "the hostages may deliberately or uncon-
sciously misrepresent the weapons held by the HT [hostage
taker]" (Fuselier, 1981:6). The hostages may even go as
far as to consciously become an advocate for the hostage
taker.

Next, Fuselier (1981:6) points out that the presence of
the Stockholm Syndrome may result in interference with
an attempt to rescue the hostages. Paradoxically, hostages'
deaths have resulted from situations in which the hostage(s)
acted counter to the commands of the police during assault
situations. Police lives may also be put in danger as the
result of hostage insistence that the situation is under
control, which occurred in Phoenix, Arizona, when a paranoid
schizophrenic hostage taker held a TV anchorman hostage.
Though he gave up after his demands were broadcast, the
situation was still dangerous because his gun, though he
had put it down on the table, was within reach. The anchorman trusted his captor so completely that he insisted that
police not rush in to handcuff the hostage taker and remove
the gun.

Fuselier (1981:6) also notes that since the Stockholm Syndrome does not always develop, those hostages who are
extremely frightened or mistreated by their captor(s) have
been known to exaggerate their plight in hopes that the
police would act sooner to attempt to rescue them. As
was indicated earlier, such assaults on the part of the police
may be more costly than one might expect and lives may
be lost needlessly in such situations.

Finally, the police negotiator may be affected by a similar
type of transference process. As Fuselier puts it, "If after
hours of attempting to build rapport and establish trust,
it becomes evident that an assault is necessary, it may
be emotionally difficult for the negotiator to distract the
HT during the initiation of an assault" (1981:6). For this
reason it is extremely advantageous to have a secondary

negotiator monitoring the negotiation process in order to be alert to the inception of this reverse transference process.

Another disadvantage and a true dilemma for law enforcement personnel confronted with a hostage situation is the fact that the Stockholm Syndrome takes time to develop. Olin and Born indicate that law enforcement officials have concluded that "the longer the incident is prolonged, the greater the probability of safe resolution, provided the hostage(s) and hostage taker(s) have interacted safely during this time period" (1983:20). In fact, one of the general guidelines in hostage negotiating is to stall for time to let the situation stabilize to decrease the intensity of emotions and to allow the Stockholm Syndrome to take effect. Stalling for time, however, may in the long run lead to severe stress-related psychological damage to the hostages. Miller states, "The longer the exposure to stress, the greater the prospect of long-term psychological damage to the victim" (1980:52). Such damage can have severe repercussions affecting all segments of the individual's life. Further, the alienation generated toward the authorities as a result of transference may then be fostered by long-term dissatisfaction with the means employed by the police in stalling. It is reasoned that the delay in police action produced the individual's protracted psychological difficulties. Thus, police personnel may again be confronted with a no-win situation.

In summary, the major dilemma presented to the police with regard to the Stockholm Syndrome is whether the probability of saving lives may be worth risking long-term severe psychological damage to hostages who do survive the hostage ordeal. Knowing that assault will likely lead to injury or loss of life, it seems that waiting in hopes that the transference process will reach the stage where the hostage taker will have built strong feelings of attachment to the hostages that will ultimately lead to their physical safety is the most ethically acceptable alternative. As has been indicated, there is no certainty that the Stockholm

Syndrome will develop, so a major portion of the dilemma is simply lack of predictability. The only way that predictability can be maximized is through excellent gathering of intelligence about the situation and the participants, and closely monitoring any interactions between the hostages and their captor. There is also a need for further scientific study of the process of transference in order to acquire knowledge that will maximize our understanding of this phenomena and increase our ability to predict its occurrence.

Politics and Hostage Negotiations

It is easy to say that, "there is no room for politics in hostage negotiation situations." It should be obvious that the moral obligation of the police in such situations should be to protect the lives of hostages, insure the safety of police personnel and to save the lives of the hostage takers. However, when the negotiation process is discussed, a number of issues are consistently raised. For example, should police strategies be in any way determined by who the hostages are? If the President, a governor, or some community leader were taken hostage, should the police respond any differently than if the hostage were an ordinary citizen? The answer to this question seems to be that there should be no difference in the police response. However, media reaction may differ if important, well-known citizens are taken hostage. Since such an occurrence would receive more publicity, its deterrent effect on potential hostage takers could be greater. This is especially true when the hostage takers are terrorists who are seeking not only that their demands are met, but also sensationalist news coverage to draw attention to their cause. It is suggested that for the sake of deterring future hostage incidents that the police maintain a consistent stance of not giving in to major demands, thus not giving in to extortion. Although the news media are obligated to keep the public informed, there also seems to be a moral obligation that they not play into the hands of those who would use innocent people, regardless of their rank or station, in order to have demands met or to gain publicity. Though the media should present the facts as they become aware of them, they should also point out the immoral nature of the acts committed by those who employ inexcusable means to achieve ends which they believe morally correct.[7]

Another question which might be asked is, should the identity of the hostage takers make a difference as to how the police respond to them. The answer here also seems to be no. Individuals should not in any way be excused from committing immoral acts because of who they are. Closely related to this is the question of motives. Again, no motive, regardless of the ultimate intent, can justify endangering the lives of innocent people. With a truly free democratic society there are many ways to make a valid cause known or to expose inequities or injustices without threatening innocent people (i.e., picketing, demonstrating or even committing acts of civil disobedience).

In summary, those involved in the hostage situation, either the hostages or the hostage taker(s) should have no effect on the goal that the police espouse as they approach the hostage situation. The dynamics of the situation, itself, in terms of the physical and mental condition of the hostages and/or the hostage taker(s) must be taken into account and will affect police decisions on a minute-by-minute basis. If the situation deteriorates (e.g., a depressed hostage taker seems to be acting out a suicide ritual) and the hostage(s) appear to be in immediate and grave danger, the police may be forced into an assault position. Even at this point the notion of accepting a certain level of casualties as part of the operation, as in the military, should not be a consideration. The goal must still be to get all individuals out alive.

When Negotiations Fail

If negotiations fail or if the police believe that hostages are being killed or are in immediate danger of losing their lives at the hands of the hostage taker(s), it may become necessary to assault. With some luck and quality police intelligence work the command staff should have detailed information about the layout of the structure in which the hostage taker and the hostages are barricaded. Further, the police should know (assuming it is possible) exactly where the hostages are located in the structure, the kind of weapon(s) possessed by the hostage taker(s) and other tactical information all of which should improve the probability of success for the assault. Knowing that an assault is likely to result in death to the hostage taker(s), hostages or police personnel, everything possible must be done to minimize this possibility. For example, when police stormed the barricaded room at St. Jude's Hospital (Memphis, TN) where Jean Claude Goulet held three people hostage, the first officer to burst into the room made a diving attempt to shield the two women hostages. The T.A.C.T. unit officer who was the designated shooter came in immediately behind him and pushed a doctor out of his way. Shots were then fired and the hostage taker, who had been wrestling with the doctor over his 357 magnum revolver was killed. No one else was hurt. The hostages after approximately 32 hours of captivity were safe, with the only injury being to the doctor whose shoulder was separated in his scuffle with Goulet.[8]

The use of deadly force in this situation was precipitated by police information obtained over the telephone through the hostages and by means of other listening devices that the situation had significantly deteriorated and that the hostage taker's psychological state was such that the hostages were in imminent danger. Had the doctor successfully wrestled the gun away from the hostage taker by the time the police broke in there would have been no casualties. Unfortunately this was not the case and the police had to confront the armed, suicidal hostage taker and they responded in the only way that was practical in order to save the hostages and themselves. Ideally such a situation should never occur, but ideal and real are unfortunately two different things.

Conclusion

Because of the variety of circumstances, motivations and personality types that can be involved in hostage situations, it is difficult to offer ethical guidelines that can be applied uniformly to all hostage situations. Guidelines to be used in the actual negotiation process have been outlined extensively elsewhere [e.g., never make concessions without getting something in return, keep the hostage taker making decisions, do not negotiate for transportation thus allowing the situation to become mobile, etc. (See, Fuselier, 1981)]. The present discussion has attempted to focus on both practical and ethical aspects of how police should respond to hostage situations. After reviewing the four types of hostage situations and elements requiring different considerations to be taken into account by police, five different response strategies to hostage situations were examined. The goal in all situations is their resolution with no harm coming to either the hostages, hostage taker(s) police, or bystanders. To do so the police must achieve meaningful dialogue with the hostage takers using the minimum amount of deception. The use of lies or forms of deception are seen as acceptable and morally excusable because the hostage taker does not have a right to expect the truth and in many situations the hostage taker is suffering from sufficient impairment of his reasoning ability so as not to accurately perceive reality. It is, however, morally incumbent upon police to employ deception as little as possible.

The advantages and disadvantages of the Stockholm Syndrome or the process of transference were also examined. It was concluded that though there can be negative long-term consequences as a result of this process being activated, the immediate safety for the hostages and the increased likelihood for successful resolution of the hostage incident brought on by the captors developing positive feelings for the hostages make police efforts to foster the occurrence of the Stockholm Syndrome morally acceptable.

Finally, it was concluded that politics should not enter into the police strategy in response to hostage situations. That is, generally, the identity of either the hostages or the hostage takers should not affect how the police approach the situation from a general strategical outlook. Specifics such as the mental or physical condition of the hostages or hostage takers must be considered and weighed carefully in the determination of negotiation or assault possibilities.

Two recommendations can be made which will, it is believed, lead to more successful and moral resolutions of hostage situations in the future. First, a great deal more research needs to be done on the dynamics of the hostage situations and, second, more training of police on responsible techniques needs to be achieved. Further, after hostage situations are resolved, thorough documentation should be provided and procedures reviewed in an attempt to discover flaws in existing policy and procedures and modifications made for future implementation.

ENDNOTES

1. For the purposes of the current discussion, ethics is used in the applied sense of "what constitutes right and wrong behavior in certain situations" (Pollock-Byrne, 1989:4). More specifically in this context ethics relates to standards of proper behavior for members of the law enforcement profession. Space limitations preclude an elaborate discussion of law enforcement ethics in general. For additional discussion of this issue see Pollock-Byrne (1989).

2. The term "Stockholm Syndrome" originated as a result of a bank robbery in Stockholm, Sweden, on August 23, 1973 in which the transference process was first identified. During the hostage incident, one of the women hostages started to identify with one of her captors to the point that she began to fear the police and in a conversation with the prime minister, assured him that the robber would

protect the hostages from the police. The woman reportedly had sexual relations with her captor and after his incarceration married him.

3. Betz specifically states that groups like "Palestinian commando groups" cause the "most frequent and serious hostage-taking problems today" (1982:123). Terrorist type hostage situations of the type mentioned are certainly serious, but they are far from being the most frequent.

4. For the purpose of the present discussion, the general topic of deception will be the central concept of debate. Since negotiating is generally a verbal process, lying is the most common form of deception likely engaged in by police in hostage situations.

5. Based on what appears to be solely journalistic accounts, Betz states that Philadelphia Police hostage negotiating squad "had been trained to lie" (1982:123). Further, since he states that they were trained in hostage negotiating by the F.B.I., the implication is that the F.B.I. teaches and condones lying as a means of negotiating with hostage takers (1982:121).

6. Sometimes the hostage taker will not negotiate directly with the police and negotiations must go through the hostages. This occurred at St. Judes Hospital in Memphis, Tennessee in 1982, perhaps because the hostage taker was an inadequate personality with paranoid tendencies. In such a situation it is easier for police to know whether the hostages and the hostage taker are experiencing the Stockholm Syndrome, since they are communicating directly with the hostages.

7. Whether the ends sought by hostage takers are morally correct or not is irrelevant. Their choice of means in a free democratic society is morally incorrect and unacceptable.

8. This is a summary of the St. Jude's Hospital hostage taking as it was directly related to the author by Memphis, Tennessee police personnel who were on the scene.

REFERENCES

Betz, Joseph. 1982. "Moral Considerations Concerning the Police Response to Hostage Takers," in **Ethics, Public Policy and Criminal Justice,** Frederick Elliston and Norman Bowie (eds.) Cambridge, MA: Oelgeschlager, Gunn & Hain, Pubs. Inc., pp. 110-132.

Beall, M. D. 1976. "Hostage Negotiations," **Military Police Law Enforcement Journal,** Vol. 3 (3) Fall, pps. 20-27.

Bok, Sissela. 1979. **Lying: Moral Choice in Public and Private Life.** New York, NY: Vantage Books.

Bolz, Frank and Edward Hershey. 1979. **Hostage Cop.** New York, NY: Rawson, Wade Publishers, Inc.

Fuselier, G. Wayne. 1981. "A Practical Overview of Hostage Negotiations," **FBI Law Enforcement Bulletin,** (June) pp. 2-6 and (July) pp. 10-15.

International Association of Chiefs of Police. 1976. Hostage-Incident Response, IACP, Gaithersburg, MD, p. 6.

Klockars, Carl B. 1980. "The Dirty Harry Problem," **The Annals of the American Academy of Political and Social Science,** Vol. 452 (November) pp. 33-47.

Lanceley, Frederick J. 1981. "The Antisocial Personality As a Hostage-Taker," **Journal of Police Science and Administration,** Vol. 9, No. 1, pp. 28-34.

Manning, Robert A. 1985. "Lessons for all Sides in Airliner Hijacking," **U.S. News and World Report,** (December 9, 1985), pp. 30-31.

Mickolus, Edward F. 1976. "Negotiating for Hostages: A Policy Dilemma," **Orbis,** 19 (Winter 1309-1325.

Miller, Abraham H. 1980. **Terrorist and Hostage Negotiations.** Boulder, Colorado: Westview Press.

Olin, W. Ronald and David G. Born. 1983. "A Behavioral Approach to Hostage Situations," **FBI Law Enforcement Bulletin,** (January) pp. 19-24.

Pollock-Byrne, Joycelyn M. 1989. **Ethics in Crime and Justice.** Brooks/Cole Publishing, Pacific Grove, CA.

CHAPTER FOUR

THE IMPLEMENTATION OF VICTIMS' RIGHTS: A CHALLENGE FOR CRIMINAL JUSTICE PROFESSIONALS

Andrew Karmen

The victories of the victims' rights movement have led to the enactment of many pledges of fair treatment and of opportunities to participate in the criminal justice process. Evaluations are now needed to determine whether criminal justice officials and agencies are implementing these recently gained rights in good faith. Such evaluations could help to clarify continuing concerns, such as whether the system can ever be reformed to operate in the best interests of victims, how the observance of victims' rights can be guaranteed, whether all victims can be treated fairly, and how often victims might opt for non-punitive resolutions of their conflicts with offenders.

INTRODUCTION

The struggle to gain formal, legal rights has been a powerful moving force throughout history. The concept of "rights" suggests both an escape from oppression and exploitation plus an achievement of independence and autonomy. A number of social movements seeking freedom, liberation, empowerment, equality, and justice have sought greater rights for their constituencies. The most well-known include civil rights, workers' rights, students' rights, children's rights, women's rights, gay rights' and prisoners' rights movements. The victims' rights movement of the late 1970s and 1980s falls within this tradition. The underlying objective of the victims' rights movement is to assure that certain standards of fair treatment towards victims are adopted and respected as their cases are processed within the criminal justice system.

The criminal justice system is a branch of the government that routinely comes under scathing criticism from many different quarters. Conservative advocates of "law and order" find fault with its alleged permissiveness. Liberal proponents of procedural egalitarianism decry the system's apparent discriminatory inequities. Radical activists denounce the system's suspected role as an instrument of ruling class domination. Crime victims, the system's supposed "clients," "consumers," or "beneficiaries", complain that standard procedures fail on a most basic level to deliver "justice".

In recent years, the victims' movement has won a number of impressive victories in its struggle for formal rights within the criminal justice process. Some of these rights have been enacted by statutes passed on the municipal, county, and state level, often as part of a legislative package called a "Victim's Bill of Rights." Others have been derived from case law based on court decisions. In some jurisdictions, certain police chiefs, district attorneys, or judges have taken it upon themselves to grant victims certain privileges and prerogatives not required by law or precedent. (For the full scope of proposals and recent gains, see the President's Task Force, 1982; NOVA, 1988; and Stark and Goldstein, 1985).

The rights that victims have fought for - and won - have become so numerous and complex, and vary so dramatically from place to place that they need to be categorized or classified. One way to group them is by the stage or phase in the criminal justice process at which these standards of fair treatment ought to be implemented. For example, some rights of victims must be respected by the police, while others should be observed by prosecutors, judges, corrections officials, or parole boards. But a better way of grouping these new rights is by asking "At whose expense

were they gained?" Given the conflicts between individuals,
groups, and classes, the rights gained by one side strengthen
their position vis-a-vis their real or potential adversaries.
Some recently enacted rights of victims clearly were secured
to the detriment of "offenders" - or more accurately:
suspects, defendants, and prisoners. For example, under
the so-called "Son of Sam" statutes, victims in most states
are enabled to lay claim to any royalties and fees paid
by movie producers or media outlets to convicts who profit
from their notoriety by selling the rights to their "inside
story". But other rights, such as the right "to be informed"
- an obligation on the part of police departments and prosecutors' offices to keep victims posted of any progress and
developments in their cases - come at the expense of the
privileges and conveniences of criminal justice officials
and the budgets of their agencies. The most widely enacted
rights of this kind are listed Part A of Chart One. A third
group of rights that empower victims to directly participate
to some degree in the criminal justice decision-making
process, such as allocation before sentencing, may come
at the expense of "offenders" or "officials", depending
upon what victims seek as they exercise their new chance
to have some input (see Karmen, 1990). The most common
statutes of this sort are listed in Part B of Chart One.

CHART ONE: PART A

Informational Rights Gained At The Expense of Criminal
Justice Agencies and Officials

---

1) To be read one's "rights": to reimbursement of losses
- from state compensation funds, court ordered offender
restitution, insurance coverage, civil lawsuits, or tax deduc-
tions; to referrals - to counseling programs, self-help support
groups, shelters for battered women, rape crisis centers,
and other types of assistance; and to be told of one's obligations - to attend line-ups, appear in court, be cross-examined
under oath, and to be publicly identified and the subject
of media coverage.

2) To be informed of the wherabouts of the (accused) offender: at large; or   in custody (jail or prison); escaped from confinement; or released back to the community (on bail, or due to dropped and dismissed charges, or because of acquittal after a trial, or out on appeal, probation, furlough, parole, or after an expired sentence).

3) To be kept posted about key decisions: arrests, the granting of bail, rulings at evidentiary hearings, negotiated pleas, verdicts at trials, sentences, and parole board deliberations.

4) To receive assistance in the form of intercession by an official in behalf of a victim with an employer or creditor; advance notification and facilitation of court appearances; and expeditious return of recovered stolen property.

CHART ONE: PART B

Participatory Rights Gained At The Expense Either of Offenders   (Suspects/Defendants/Convicts)   or   Agencies and Officials

---

1) To be consulted when the terms and conditions of bail are being determined (as a protection against harassment and reprisals for cooperating with the prosecution).

2) To be consulted about the offers made during plea negotiations.

3) To be permitted to submit a victim impact statement, detailing how the crime caused physical, emotional, and/or financial harm, as part of the pre-sentence report, and to submit a statement of opinion suggesting remedies, for the judge's consideration.

4) To be permitted to exercise allocation rights in person, in court, detailing the harm caused by the offender and

suggesting an appropriate remedy, before the judge imposes
a sentence.

5) To be permitted to bring to the attention of the parole
board, either in writing or in person, information about
the harm caused by the offender and an opinion about an
appropriate remedy.

Source: Karmen, 1990.

Now that a sufficient amount of time has passed since
the enactment of these rights, a growing body of data is
accumulating about their implementation - or lack of observance - and evaluations are underway (for example, see
NIJ, 1989). In fact, legislation introduced before Congress
in 1989 called upon the Department of Justice to conduct
an annual evaluation of the extent of compliance of federal
agencies with the provisions of the Victim and Witness
Protection Act of 1982 and the Victims of Crime Act of
1984 ("Bi-partisan Victim Rights Bill," 1989). Thus, it is
time to anticipate how the results of these evaluations
of pledges about fair treatment might be compiled and
interpreted to answer some classical questions that persist
within the disciplines of criminal justice, criminology,
and victimology.

The findings of evaluation studies, as they accumulate,
might either undermine or else lend support to some long-
standing suspicions and criticisms about the ways that
the criminal justice system operates. It seems worthwhile
to hypothesize and speculate about what researchers might
discover. If the findings consistently fall into certain patterns, well-grounded answers will emerge for the following
questions:

**Whose interests are primarily served by the routine opera-
tions of the criminal justice system?**

The idealistic answer to this question is that the system primarily serves the interests of the whole society in general, and crime victims in particular. Of course, there are many other legitimate sources of input into the decision-making process, and victims are just one of many interested parties. But if indeed victims are truly the clients, customers, consumers, and beneficiaries of a system ostensibly set up to deliver justice to them, then evidence should accumulate that officials and agencies concede their right to participate in the decision-making process. Evaluations should show that victims feel satisfied that their needs and wants were taken into account by decision-makers, even if their requests did not prevail; and that although they were not always "catered to" or "handled with care", they were treated with dignity, respect, and fundamental fairness.

The skeptical, more sociological answer to this question is that a displacement of goals occurs within bureaucratic settings. Unofficial goals, such as minimizing collective effort and maximizing individual and group rewards might be substituted for the official goals of dispensing justice, aiding victims, and serving the public interest. In the context of criminal justice agencies, the hidden agenda behind many official actions might be to dispose of cases in a manner that lightens workloads, covers up mistakes, and curries political favors (McDonald, 1979). Since criminal justice professionals are not directly accountable to victims, either legally or organizationally, they can be inclined to view victims as a resource to be drawn upon, as needed, in the pursuit of objectives such as maintaining high levels of productivity in case processing, and in achieving smooth coordination with other components of the system (Ziegenhagen, 1977). When minor inconveniences to insiders (such as prosecutors, defense attorneys, judges, probation officers, and parole board members) have to be balanced against major inconveniences to outsiders (victims, defendants, witnesses, jurors), insider interests prevail (Ash, 1972). For instance, the courtroom work group of insiders develops a consensus about the "going rate" of appropriate penalties for particular crimes at a given time and place. This work group composed primarily of prosecutors, defense attorneys, and judges tends to resist attempts by outsiders and reformers to alter the penalty structure and disrupt their assembly line processing of cases (Walker, 1989). To the extent that the courtroom workgroup is successful in maintaining their standard operating procedures, victims will find their attempts to influence sentencing (or bail determinations, or plea negotiations, or parole deliberations) an exercise in futility. Their efforts to become involved in the decision-making process will be rebuffed as an intrusion, interference, and a threat to jealously guarded and highly prized professional discretionary authority (see Ranish and Shichor, 1985).

Some preliminary evidence already supports this prediction of "more of the same." Researchers who evaluated the use by victims of their right (since 1982) to allocation in felony cases in California confirmed its ineffectiveness. Plea negotiations which resulted in dismissals of all felony charges or in an understanding of what the sentence would be eliminated the chance for many victims to have any meaningful say in determining the outcomes of their cases. Determinate sentencing laws further eroded victim input. In many cases, officials failed to inform victims of their rights; some of the remaining eligible victims forfeited their chance to appear because of a belief that their appearance before the judge would make no difference in shaping a sentence that was already decided. Of those who exercised their opportunity for allocation, a considerable number felt their recommendations were not heeded. In the opinion of the majority of probation officers and judges, and about half of the prosecutors surveyed, the personal appearances by victims were "minimally, or not at all effective" (Villmoare and Neto, 1987). Similar findings about the difficulty victims have experienced in trying to influence the decision-making process appeared in evaluations of "structured" plea negotiation experiments. Victims who were permitted to attend the negotiation conferences tended to conclude that their presence and the statements they made had no impact on case disposition (Heinz and Kerstetter, 1979; Villmoare and Neto, 1987).

Are some victims more equal than others?

Evaluations might uncover great disparities in the way victims are treated by officials and agencies. A relatively small percentage of privileged people harmed by street criminals might enjoy "first class," "red carpet," or "VIP" treatment - their rights are scrupulously observed - while socially disadvantaged persons experience mistreatment as "second-class complainants." Such a blatant double-standard of justice is not supposed to develop because it violates official doctrines and constitutional guarantees subsumed under the clause "Equal protection under the law", and the pledge, "And justice for all." But many previous studies of case processing indicate that victim characteristics can influence outcomes like decisions to arrest, prosecute, convict, and severely punish offenders (see Myers, 1977; Myers and Hagan, 1979; Paternoster, 1984; Farrell and Swigert, 1986; and Karmen, 1990).

What if evaluations demonstrate that certain categories of victims are more likely to be informed by officials and are more likely to exercise their participatory rights, with demonstrably favorable results? Will the discriminatory treatment in the implementation of informational rights - and especially participatory rights - be correlated with victim characteristics such as race/ethnicity; gender; age; and social class (financial standing; educational attainment; occupational status; reputation in the community)? To state the matter bluntly, will victims drawn from the "right" backgrounds receive better service from the criminal justice system than the vast bulk of underprivileged people routinely preyed upon by street criminals?

Of course, the evaluations might uncover differential treatment on the basis of other factors, as well, which could stimulate considerable debate between officials and victims advocates. For example, should assault victims with "unsavory" backgrounds, such as street gang members, drug abusers, gamblers, and prostitutes be granted the same privileges concerning information and participation as totally innocent, law-abiding victims drawn from other walks of life? If they receive perfunctory responses when they turn to the system for help, would it be justifiable because they are assumed to be offenders in other incidents? Should surrogates and advocates who represent victimized children, and should survivors of murder victims exercise the same rights as direct victims?

What happens when criminal justice professionals violate the rights of crime victims?

The evaluations might expose a thorny problem. What recourse do victims have when their informational and participatory rights are violated? Anticipating the possibility that agencies and officials might fail to inform and involve victims as promised, legislators in many states crafted into their "Victims' Bills of Rights" clauses stating that "nothing in this statute shall be construed as creating a cause of action against the state, a county, municipality, or any of its agents." However, under the separation of powers doctrine, judges might direct officials and agencies to honor their commitments and could authorize injunctive relief for victims who file lawsuits (Stark and Goldstein, 1985). If evaluations turn up widespread non-compliance, additional remedies will be demanded.

Besides inadequate mechanisms for enforcement, evaluations might highlight another related problem: the absence of clear lines of responsibility for implementation. Several different officials and agencies might be held accountable for respecting victims rights. For example, the duty of notifying complainants who served as witnesses for the prosecution of their right to allocation before sentencing might fall to the police, the district attorney's office, the probation department, or a clerk in the office of court administration. All sorts of unanticipated complications might come to light. For example, how many attempts to contact the victim must be made (by phone or mail or in person) before the responsible official can declare that a good faith effort was undertaken to inform and involve the victim in plea negotiations, sentencing recommendations, or parole board deliberations?

Are victims invariably punitive toward offenders?

It is anticipated from common stereotypes, widespread assumptions, and some survey findings (see Hernon and Forst, 1984) that the vast majority of victims will use their newly gained influence to press for the most punitive sanctions permitted under the law. But a significant proportion (how often and under what circumstances?) might argue against lengthy confinement of convicts if alternatives are available. Those victims who do not seek the system's help to exact revenge might expect criminal justice professionals to treat and rehabilitate the persons who harmed them, especially if the offenders are former friends, acquaintances, or relatives. Other victims might place a higher priority on being reimbursed through offender restitution as a condition of probation and parole. Some preliminary reports indicate that when victims are given a full range of options, a significant fraction favor restitution, rehabilitation, and reconciliation over retribution (see Galaway, 1985; Villmoare and Neto, 1987; and Umbreit, 1989).

In conclusion, it is clear that the implementation of victims' rights poses a challenge to criminal justice professionals, especially police administrators, district attorneys, probation officers, judges, corrections officials, and parole board members. How they respond, as revealed by evaluation research, to the demands by victims for fair treatment will resolve many controversies and provoke new ones.

REFERENCES

Ash, M. 1972. "On witnesses: A radical critique of criminal court procedures." Notre Dame Lawyer, 48 (December), pp. 386-425.

"Bi-partisan victim rights bill introduced in U.S. Congress." 1989. NOVA Newsletter 13, 3, pp. 1, 5.

Farrell, R. and Swigert, V. 1986. "Adjudication in homicide: An interpretive analysis of the effects of defendant and victim social characteristics." Journal of Research in Crime and Delinquency 23, 4 (November), pp. 349-369.

Galaway, B. 1985. "Victim participation in the penal-correction process." Victimology 10, 1, pp. 617-629.

Hernon, J. and Forst, B. 1984. NIJ Research in brief: The criminal justice response to victim harm. Washington, D.C.: U.S. Department of Justice.

Heinz. A. and Kerstetter, W. 1979. "Pretrial settlement conference: Evaluation of a reform in plea bargaining." Law and Society Review, 13, 2, pp. 349-366.

Karmen, A. 1990. Crime Victims: An introduction to victimology. Second edition. Pacific Grove, Ca.: Brooks/Cole.

McDonald, W. 1979. "The prosecutor's domain." In W. McDonald (Ed.), The prosecutor (pp. 15-52). Beverly Hills, Ca.: Sage.

Myers, M. 1977. The effects of victim characteristics on the prosecution, conviction, and sentencing of criminal defendants. Ann Arbor, Mi.: University Microfilms.

_____ and Hagan, J. 1979. "Private and public trouble: Prosecutors and the allocation of court resources." Social Problems, 26, 4, pp. 439-451.

National Institute of Justice (NIJ). 1989. Research in action: The courts- current federal research. Washington, D.C.: U.S. Department of Justice.

National Organization for Victim Assistance (NOVA). 1988. Victim rights and services: A legislative directory - 1987. Washington, D.C.: Author.

Paternoster, R. 1984. "Prosecutorial discretion in requesting the death penalty: A case of victim based racial discrimination." Law and Society Review, 18, 437-478.

President's Task Force on Victims of Crime. 1982. Final Report. Washington, D.C.: U.S. Government Printing Office.

Ranish, D. and Shichor, D. 1985. "The victim's role in the penal process: Recent developments in California." Federal Probation (March), pp. 50-56.

Stark, J. and Goldstein, H. 1985. The rights of crime victims. Chicago: Southern Illinois University Press.

Umbreit, M. 1989. "Violent offenders and their victims." In M. Wright and B. Galaway (Eds.), Mediation and criminal justice: Victims, offenders, and community (pp. 99-112). Newbury Park, Ca.: Sage.

Villmoare, E. and Neto, V. 1987. NIJ Research in brief: Victim appearances at sentencing under California's victims' bill of rights. Washington, D.C.: U.S. Department of Justice.

Walker, S. 1989. Sense and nonsense about crime: A policy guide. (Second edition). Pacific Grove, Ca.: Brooks/Cole.

Ziegenhagen, E. 1977. Victims, crime, and social control. New York: Praeger.

CHAPTER FIVE

THE INTERACTIONIST APPROACH TO
TO CRIME AND CORRECTIONS

Leroy C. Gould

and

Susan L. Sayles

Corrections like criminology has been dominated throughout this century in the United States by an "offender-oriented" view of crime. This article argues that a new interactionist perspective on crime is emerging in criminology and that this new "social-event" view of crime has implications for corrections. In particular, it argues that traditional correctional notions about treatment and rehabilitation, deterrence, punishment, retribution, and social defense may either have to be modified or abandoned.

INTRODUCTION

Corrections, like the criminological theory from which it draws, reflects a culture's views of human nature (cf. Erikson 1966: 183-206). It is not surprising, therefore, that as American optimism waned in the 1970's (Lipset et al., 1983), American criminology became more pessimistic (Martinson, 1974; Ehrlich, 1974; Wilson, 1975), and the focus of corrections switched from treatment and rehabilitation (Joint Commission, 1968) to security and punishment.

Argument continues over which is the better correctional philosophy (Wilson and Herrnstein, 1985). Since these arguments rest upon opposing, deeply-held, and probably untestable views of human nature, it might seem that corrections is destined to periodic, and perhaps never-ending, shifts of purpose and objectives.

Recent trends in criminological theory suggest a way out of this dilemma. Specifically, recent criminiological theory has been shifting away from a focus on individual offenders to a focus on crime itself. This shift could provide a theoretical means for avoiding criminological and correctional arguments about human nature. The purpose of this paper is to review these recent trends and to speculate about their implications for corrections.

HISTORICAL PERSPECTIVE

During the first half or more of this century, theories of crime by American Criminolgists focused on the behavior of criminals (Jeffery, 1959; Matza, 1964). That is, they addressed the question: why do people commit crimes? In recent years, at least four major theories of crime have emerged that are not dominated by this subject. One, critical criminology focuses on the law and those who administer the law (Hopkins, 1975). Critical criminology, thereby, has revived interest in questions that preoccupied classical European criminologists about the nature and administration of law (Jeffery, 1959). Labeling theory, which developed at about the same time, is concerned primarily with societal reactions to perceived deviance (Becker, 1973). Rules, and the application of rules, therefore are the focus of this criminological tradition. Economic theory (Becker, 1968; Ehrlich, 1981), which presupposes a utilitarian human nature, emphasizes the deterrent affects of criminal-justice sanctions. The focus of economic theory, therefore, is not the offender, but enforcement agents and agencies. Opportunity theory,[1] the most recent of these theoretical developments, argues that characteristics of crime targets plays an important role in determining differential victimization and overall rates of crime (Cock, 1986). The focus of opportunity theory, therefore, is victims and criminal opportunities rather than criminal offenders.

Crimes as Social Events

That these recent criminological theories have shifted away from an emphasis on criminal behavior would seem to indicate that criminology is moving toward a conception of crime that involves more than the behavior of individual offenders. Like classical criminologists (Beccaria, 1764) American criminologists are again accepting the notion that a crime, in the first instance, involves a violation of law. Also, as critical criminolgoists, labeling theorists, and economic theorists have been pointing out, a crime also involves law-enforcement agents. And, as opportunity theory argues, crimes also involve victims and criminal opportunities. A crime, in other words, from this new perspective, is not merely the illegal behavior of an offender, but an interaction among offender(s), victim(s), and control agent(s) that occurs within a society that has defined these events as illegal (i.e. they are against the law) and has perceived on crime can be seen in the writings of a number of criminologists (Wheeler, 1967; Biderman and Reiss, 1967; Gould, 1971, Luckenbill, 1977; Cook, 1980; Ehrlich, 1981) the perspective is not universal. Neither has it received a name. For the sake of brevity, we will call it the "interactionist approach to crime."[2]

One of the more important aspects of the interactionist approach to crime is that it dissociates the concept "crime" from the behavior of offenders, thereby inviting criminologists to think of crimes, not as **individual** events but as particular kinds of **social** events; that is, as events that involve interactions among one or more offenders, one or more victims (or crime targets), and one or more agents of social control, that society has defined as criminal. Such a conceptualization draws attention to the fact that crimes, broadly speaking, involve both practical and etiological factors that go beyond the behavior of individual offenders. Such a conceptualization also provides a method of unifying several heretofore seemingly disparate, and sometimes even contentious, criminological traditions. The conceptualization is quite consistent with labeling theory, critical criminology, deterrence theory, and opportunity theory (indeed, it grew in large part from these traditions). It is also congruous with more traditional American positivists approaches to crime in that it acknowledges that offenders are one component of crimes, and indeed, does not preclude the proposition, as utilitarian economic theory does (Becker, 1968), that differences in criminality (i.e. differences in the propensity to commit crimes) may in fact make a difference in overall rates of crime.

IMPLICATIONS FOR CORRECTIONS

Although professionals in corrections differ about the importance of each, most would agree that the correctional system, at least to some extent, performs each of the following functions: deterrence, punishment, retribution, social defense, and treatment or rehabilitation (Wilson and Herrnstine, 1985: 492-498). In a 1968 survey (Joint Commission) a majority of correctional personnel cited treatment and rehabilitation as the primary goals of the system. This emphasis came surely from the overwhelming emphasis in American criminology during those years on the study of criminal behavior. If the crime problem is primarily attributable to criminal behavior, its solution would appear to lie, most logically, in modifying this behavior.

The interactionist approach to crime does not assume that the crime problem is only, or even primarily, a matter of criminal behavior. Since crimes also involve the behavior of victims, social control agents, and society at large, any of these other actors may be as important in the etiology of crime as the offender himself or herself. In other words, if individual human criminal behavior is only part of the problem, modifying individual criminal motivations may be only part of the solution. What does the empirical evidence suggest?

Treatment and Rehabilitation

In 1975, Lipton, Martinson, and Wilks published the results of a lengthy review of over 200 controlled evaluations of correctional treatment programs. They found that while some forms of treatment, particularly education and job training, tended to have positive results, and others, particularly those based on psychotherapy, tended to have negative results, no form of treatment had very large or very consistent effects. Although some people interpreted these conclusions to mean that "nothing works" (Martinson, 1974), a more prudent interpretation would be "that nothing tried so far has worked very well or very consistently." But this is exactly what the interactionist approach to crime would predict: if criminality is only one of several causal factors in crime, programs designed to reduce criminality, even if they are successful programs, will have only a limited impact on crime itself.

Deterrence

What about deterrence? Even though correctional programs may have little impact on the future criminal behavior of those persons they process, might not correctional programs, by their very existence, deter people who have not committed crimes from attempting them in the first place?

The evidence here is also equivocal. Although some macro-level deterrence studies have found length of imprisonment and capital punishment to be negatively correlated with the incidence of some kinds of crime, other studies have found no correlation between measures of punishment severity and rates of crime (cf. Blumstein et al., 1978). Individual-level studies, that is studies that ask people directly about their perceptions of punishment severity and their criminal misconduct, have also found punishment severity either not to be correlated with misconduct or to be correlated with it only weakly and inconsistently (Paternoster et al., 1983).

If prisons neither correct very well nor deter very much, do they fulfill any of their other functions any better? Empirical evidence cannot answer this question since no study presently known has ever tried to measure how well prisons punish, mete out retribution, or protect society. The interactionist approach to crime, however, might shed some light on how well we might expect corrections to fulfill these objectives.[3]

Punishment

Punishment, of course, is closely associated with deterrence; it is fear of punishment that presumably deters crime. But, punishment involves more than deterrence. Punishment also involves a community's sense of justice.

Most people feel that a person who has committed a wrong should suffer some pain as a consequence of that action. This belief holds whether or not anyone has been seriously hurt by the wrong or whether punishment would necessarily serve to deter further wrongs of the same kind. It is simply that people seem to find it immoral for anyone to get by without being punished when they have violated rules that the community holds to be important. Punishing wrongdoers is a means, then, of meting out justice.

The severity of punishment, in other words, is one way a society has of saying how wrong it feels a certain action is. When Beccaria (1764) and other classical criminologists argued that the punishment should "fit the crime," they were only in part arguing that the punishment should be severe enough to deter the crime; they were also arguing that the punishment should define the seriousness of the crime. Later sociologist, in particular Durkheim (1950 and 1960) and Erikson (1966), developed this point at some length, arguing that it is through the use of punishment that a society defines and maintains its normative order. It is on this point, however, that treatment-oriented correctional programs run into one of their biggest problems.

One of the prerequisites of good treatment is that different people may be treated differently. As a rule, however, there is little correspondence between the kind of treatment a particular offender might require and the kind of crime she or he might have committed. A murderer, for example, is a good parole risk (Giardini and Farrow, 1952) and a drunk a poor one (Pittman and Gordon, 1958) yet most Americans probably would not find it fair to keep a drunk in prison longer than a murderer.

To the extent, then, that the demands of treatment do not correspond to a community's demands for justice, a correctional system finds it hard either to administer effective treatment or to fulfill its obligations to define and maintain the normative order. Since the normative order, from the interactionist point of view, is just as important as the behavior of offenders, and since correctional institutions do not seem to be able to treat very well anyway, the interactionist approach to crime would argue that correctional programs probably should not sacrifice the community's sense of justice for a dubious commitment to treatment. In the long run, maintaining a strong normative system may be just as important in the war on crime as maintaining a law-abiding citizenry.

Retribution

The urge to retaliate against someone who has caused pain, suffering, or loss of property seems to be universal. While an "eye for an eye" does not restore sight nor does a "life for a life" bring back life, thus rendering the penchant for revenge irrational, rationality is not always uppermost in human relations, and at times the forces of rationality and irrationality conflict.

In most nations today, the institutions of social control do not deny the desire for revenge. They do, however, try to control it. They control it, first of all, by establishing time-consuming legal procedures. (Since the impulse for revenge, be it on the part of the offender or the community at large, is immediate, protracted proceedings give time for passions to subside.) They also control it by no longer allowing an offended party to be the agent who executes criminal sanctions against the offender.

Although the public monopolization of retribution denies the lust for private revenge, it has a number of long-range advantages. Unbridled private revenge often leads to interminable vendettas. In a vendetta, the circle of accomplices tends to widen and the demands for vengeance often escalate. The loss of a purse will demand the mutilation of a hand which leads to the loss of an eye, the taking of a life, and total havoc, while the wider community is torn asunder.

While it is not altogether necessary that retribution and rehabilitation be incompatible, correctional personnel often argue that they are (President's Crime Commission, 1967). To the extent that they are right, providing good treatment within the correctional system and maintaining society's probably rather tenuous monopoly on retribution are in conflict. Doing one well may mean doing the other poorly.

Social Defense

While offenders may return to a life of crime after being incarcerated, spending time in jail and prison at least spares society those crimes the offenders would have committed had they not been locked away. Or at least so it would seem. This common wisdom will be true, however, only if it is also true that those who are incarcerated are not replaced in the criminal marketplace by other offenders. It will be true, in other words, only if the total volume of crime at any one time is a function only of the total number of people at that time who are motivated to commit crimes. It will not be true if the total number of crimes at any one time is also a function of the opportunities to commit crimes.

The interactionist approach to crime posits that the total number of crimes in any one time or place will be a function, not only of varying levels of motivation in the population to commit crimes, but also of varying levels of opportunity to commit crimes of various kinds and of levels of law-enforcement activity and effectiveness. Among these three factors, some studies have found opportunities to be very important, particularly under certain economic conditions (Gould, 1969 and 1971).

The interactionist approach to crime, then, would argue that incarceration is not a good method of social defense; that locking criminals away does not reduce the total volume of crime very much since it opens up criminal opportunities for other people, some of whom would not have engaged in crime had these opportunities not existed. The net result will not be significantly less crime, although it will be significantly more criminals.

The Disease Model of Crime and Corrections

One of the results of conceiving of crimes as the acts of individual persons, rather than as social units or the interactions of several persons, is that the notion emerges that crime, like mental illness or alcoholism, must be some kind of disease. Although many people have praised this notion as being humanitarian and progressive, others, including sociologists, lawyers, and psychologists, have questioned the usefulness of this kind of "disease" model of crime (Lemert, 1951; Szasz, 1961; Goffman, 1961; Matza, 1964; Kittrie, 1971).

The interactionist approach to crime does not assume that offenders are sick (although some persons who are sick may commit crimes as a result of their illnesses). Instead, it assumes that criminals, for the most part, are probably pretty much like noncriminals. What separates the two groups has more to do with one group's opportunities to commit crimes and with the behavior of society's agents of social control toward them than it does with either their biology or their psychology.

The interactionist approach also does not assume that crime is a "social" disease. As Durkheim (1950) argued, particularly high or particularly low rates of crime may be **symptomatic** of social distress (the crime rate, for example, is never so low as in times of war), but crime **per se** is not a social pathology. Rather it is one of the regular, ongoing, and perhaps even necessary aspects of a dynamic, advancing society.

The role of corrections, then, from the interactionist perspective, is neither to cure criminals nor to eliminate crime; it is, rather, along with other components of the criminal-justice system like the police and criminal courts, to administer justice. Justice in this context, however, is neither repression nor subjugation, but rather, is the expression of community standards. It is not setting longer and longer sentences under the misguided notion that this will deter crime, but setting fair sentences that will reflect the community's sense of how serious different kinds of offenses are. It is not building more and more prisons under the misguided notion that this will protect society, but increasing the legitimate alternatives to criminal careers and working to decrease the number of criminal opportunities in the community. To the extent, in other words, that correctional and other criminal justice institutions administer **justice** well, they will have done their jobs well, quite irrespective of how successful they may have been in "curing" its inmates of "criminality" or deterring potential offenders.

CONCLUSIONS

The interactionists approach to crime reminds us that no institution exists in a cultural or historical vacuum. Corrections, therefore, cannot solve the "crime problem" alone. It can, however, by doing its part to administer justice fairly, help to create a cultural environment that may in the long run contribute to a more law-abiding citizenry.

To the extent that treatment and rehabilitation further these goals, there is no reason to exclude these activities from the correctional system. To the extent that they conflict with the community's sense of justice, however, they are probably best left to other institutions. (It is a sad commentary on the overall system of care providing in our country that people often have to be convicted of a crime before help is made available to them.) At the very least, treatment and rehabilitation probably should be emphasized more as a part of probation and parole, with which they are more compatible, than with incarceration.

There are also, of course, alternatives to conventional incarceration, including, among others, work release and house arrest. (Among the newest are electronic surveillance systems whereby officers of the court can monitor the activities of convicted offenders). These systems, however, depend on an "offender-oriented" conception of crime, and as such are no more likely than traditional correctional programs to affect overall rates of crime. In contrast, the interactionist approach to crime argues for a "criminal-event" conception that perceives of crimes as only in part a function of what offenders do. Of equal importance are what victims, agents of social control, and society as a whole does. What corrections can do to affect these other agents in the crime process is not altogether clear, but time and a conception of crime that does not focus so narrowly on offenders might serve as the catalyst for such ideas.

ENDNOTES

1. The term "opportunity theory," in this context, should not be confused with "differential opportunity theory" as proposed earlier by Merton (1938), Cloward and Ohlin

(1960) and others. Although there are some logical connections between the two theoretical traditions (see for example Cook, 1986: 2-3), the focus of opportunity theory is on potential crime victims while the focus of differential opportunity theory (usually called "strain theory") is on potential offenders.

2. Howard Becker (1975: 177-208) suggested that "interactionist-perspective" would be a better term than "labeling" to describe his and other labeling theorist's work. Our use of the term "interactionist" then, in some ways is an extension of the interactionist perspective suggested by Becker.

3. The following discussion derives in part from Gould and Namenwirth (1971).

REFERENCES

Beccaria, Cesare. 1764. **Essay on Crimes and Punishments.** (For a more recent U.S. publication, see Indianapolis: Bobbs-Merrill, 1963.)

Becker, Gary. 1968. "Crime and Punishment: An Economic approach," **Journal of Political Economy** 78: 169-217.

Becker, Howard. 1973. **Outsiders.** New York: Free Press.

Blumstein, Alfred, Jacqueline Cohen, and David Nagin (eds.). 1978. **Deterrence and Incapacitation: Estimating the Effects of Criminal Sanctions on Crime Rates.** Washington D.C.: National Academy of Sciences.

Cook, Philip J. 1980. "Research in Criminal Deterrence: Laying the Groundwork for the Second Decade." In Norval Morris and Michael Tonry (eds.) **Crime and Justice: An Annual Review of Research,** vol. 2. Chicago: University of Chicago Press.

Cook, Philip J. 1986. "The Demand and Supply of Criminal Opportunities. In Michael Tonry and Norvil Morris (eds.) **Crime and Justice: An Annual Review of Research,** vol. 7. Chicago: University of Chicago Press.

Durkheim, Emile. 1950. **Rule of the Sociological Method,** tr. by Sarah Salvay and John Mueller and ed. by George Catlin, New York: Free Press.

Durkheim, Emile. 1960. **The Division of Labor in Society,** tr. by George Simpson. New York: Free Press.

Ehrlich, Issaac. 1974. "Participating in Illegitimate Activities: An Economic Analysis." In Gary S. Becker and William M. Landes (eds.) **Essays in the Economics of Crime and Punishment.** New York: Columbia University Press.

Ehrlich, Issaac. 1981. "On the Usefulness of Controlling Individuals: An Economic Analysis of Rehabilitation, Incapacitation, and Deterrence," **American Economic Review,** 71: 307-322.

Erikson, Kai T. 1966. **Wayward Puritans: A Study in the Sociology of Deviance.** New York: Wiley.

Giardini, G. I. and R. G. Farrow. 1952. "The Paroling of Capital Offenders," **Annals of the American Academy of Political and Social Sciences** 284: 85-94.

Goffman, Erving. 1961. **Asylums.** Garden City, New York: Doubleday.

Gould, Leroy C. 1969. "The Changing Structure of Property Crime in an Affluent Society," **Social Forces** 48: 50-59.

Gould, Leroy C. 1971. "Crime and its Impact in an Affluent Society." In Jack Douglas (ed.) **Crime and Justice in American Society,** Indianapolis: Bobbs-Merrill.

Gould, Leroy C. and J. Zvi Namenwirth. 1981. "Contrary Objectives; Crime Control and the Rehabilitation of Criminals." in Jack Douglas (ed.) **Crime and Justice in American Society,** Indianapolis: Bobbs-Merrill.

Hopkins, Andrew. 1975. "On the Sociology of Criminal Law," **Social Problems** 22: 608-619.

Jeffery, Clarence Ray. 1959. "The Historical Development of Criminology," **The Journal of Criminal Law, Criminology and Police Science** 50: 3-19. (Reprinted and expanded in Hermann Mannheim (ed.) **Pioneers in Criminology.** Montclair, New Jersey: Patterson Smith.

Joint Commission on Correctional Manpower and Training. 1968. **Corrections 1968: A Climate for Change.** Washington D.C.: 15K. St. N.W.

Kittrie, Nicholas N. 1971. **The Right to be Different: Deviance and Enforced Therapy.** Baltimore: Johns Hopkins University Press.

Lemert, Edwin M. 1951. **Social Pathology.** New York: McGraw-Hill.

Lipset, Seymour Martin, and William Schneider. 1983. **The Confidence Gap.** New York: Free Press.

Lipton, Douglas, Robert Martinson and Judith Wilks. 1975. **The Effectiveness of Correctional Treatment: A Survey of Treatment Evaluation Studies.** New York: Praeger.

Luckenbill, David. 1977. "Criminal Homicide as a Situated Transaction," **Social Problems** 25: 176-186.

Martinson, Robert. 1974. "What Works: Questions and Answers about prison reform." **Public Interest.** Spring 22-54.

Matza, David. 1964. **Delinquency and Drift.** New York: Wiley.

Paternoster, Raymond, Linda E. Saltzman, Gordon P. Waldo, and Theodore G. Chiricos. 1983. "Estimating Perceptual Stability and Deterrent Effects: The Role of Perceived Legal Punishment in the Inhibition of Criminal Involvement," **Journal of Criminal Law and Criminology** 74: 270-97.

Pittman, David J. and C. Wayne Gordon. 1958. **Revolving Door: A Study of the Chronic Police Case Inebriate.** New York: Free Press.

President's Commission on Law Enforcement and Administration of Justice (President's Crime Commission). 1967. **The Challenge of Crime in a Free Society.** Washington D.C.: U.S. Government Printing Office.

Szasz, Thomas. 1964. **The Myth of Mental Illness: Foundations of a Theory of Personal Conduct.** New York: Hoeber.

Weber, Max. 1964. **The Theory of Social and Economic Organization,** Talcot Parsons (ed.); trans. A. M. Henderson. New York: Free Press.

Wheeler, Stanton. 1967. "Criminal Statistics: A Reformulation of the Problem," **Journal of Criminal Law, Criminology and Police Science,** 58: 317-324.

Wilson, James Q. 1975. **Thinking About Crime.** New York: Basic Books.

Wilson, James Q. and Richard J. Herrnstein. 1985. **Crime and Human Nature.** New York: Simon and Schuster.

CHAPTER SIX

BOOT CAMP CORRECTIONS: A PUBLIC REACTION*

Philip L. Reichel

and

Angela Kailey Gauthier

Shock incarceration, or "boot camp corrections," is a prison alternative developed to instill a sense of discipline and respect for authority in inmates. The three to six month program of intense physical labor is used for young non-violent, first-time offenders, as an option to a regular term prison sentence. With a goal of reducing both overcrowding in prisons and recidivism, this program is attracting national attention. After describing existing boot camp programs, this study reports the results of a public opinion survey to gauge the probable response of citizens to the use of shock incarceration as a standard sentencing strategy. The study found the public to be supportive of this alternative to imprisonment and suggests that policy makers be more willing to propose and support creative options to incarceration.

INTRODUCTION

Since the 1970s, the mass media, politicians, and academicians have made reference to the "get tough on crime" philosophy embraced by American society. That philosophy

---

*This is a revised version of a paper presented at the Annual Meeting of the Academy of Criminal Justice Sciences, Washington, D.C., March 30, 1989.

oriented such policy as stiffening of sentences, lessening judicial discretion, emasculating parole boards, increasing the use of imprisonment (forcing the construction of more prisons), and a return to the use of capital punishment.

While the objective reality of those conditions cannot be ignored, the basis upon which they have been implemented may present more of a puzzle. One assumption is that since those changes are primarily the result of legislative action, we expect that in this representative democracy the legislators' votes reflect their constituents' opinions. On the other hand, some research over the last five years suggests a lack of complete concordance between public opinion and the changes in criminal justice policy toward a solely (or even primarily) punitive stance. In other words, is American society following a "get tough" philosophy because that is what the public wants, or because that is what politicians, correctional administrators, and policy makers **think** the public wants? In addition, if the "get tough" policy is interpreted as requiring imprisonment and longer sentences, it is questionable whether effective use is made of unconventional methods which the public may actually favor.

This article reports the result of research which addresses both of those problems. On the one hand, there is a concern with public attitudes regarding societal response to criminals and at the same time there is an interest in the acceptance of an alternative to imprisonment called shock incarceration or boot camp corrections. We begin with a discussion of the research on public opinion regarding correctional policy, proceed to a description of existing boot camp programs, then present the results of a survey on reaction to shock incarceration as an option to imprisonment.

The Myth of a Non-progressive Public

Immarigeon (1986) suggests that a barrier blocking the implementation of system-wide correctional reform is the apparent tough mood of current public opinion. "Legislators and criminal justice policy makers have shaped correctional policy according to what they see, or claim to see, as the public's active interest in society's being 'tough enough' in its response to the criminal offender" (Immarigeon, 1986, p. 1). Similarly, Cullen, Clark, and Wozniak comment on the perception that "current criminal justice policies are a direct reflection of the increasing salience of lawlessness for citizens and their subsequent plea that the state punish and cage the wicked" (1985, p. 16). If it is true that criminal justice policy simply reflects public desire, we are not only secure in the knowledge that our representative democracy works, but should arguably show restraint in putting forward programs which contradict those attitudes. On the other hand, if the policy does not reflect public desire, we may stifle innovation under the mistaken impression that it violates the public will. Recent studies suggest that the latter condition may be more true.

Riley and Rose (1980) tested the assumption that a representative form of government presents a situation where the public, at least indirectly, influences the decisions of public officials. The results of their work provide one of the first indications that public officials misinterpret public attitudes about punishment. They found that despite contrary views by correctional decision makers, the public had a positive attitude toward "progressive reform" rather than being predominantly punitive. The public, for example, was much more receptive to community based programs and to parole and probation than elites expected (Riley & Rose, 1980).

Four years later, Gottfredson and Taylor (1984) surveyed policy makers and the general public and found remarkable concordance of opinion between the two groups regarding the desirability of using community based options in response to prison overcrowding. The problem, however, was that policy makers perceived the public as being generally punitive and made decisions based on those misperceptions. Specifically, Gottfredson and Taylor (1984) found the general public to stress utilitarian goals (e.g., rehabilitation and deterrence) over punitive ones as did the policy makers. However, while both the public and the policy groups held attitudes characterized as rather liberal, non-punitive, utilitarian, and reform oriented, the policy group attributed almost the reverse to the public. The authors refer to this predicament as an example of pluralistic ignorance wherein persons underestimate the extent to which others share the beliefs and sentiments which they themselves hold (Gottfredson & Taylor, 1984, p. 196).

Cullen, et al. (1985) emphasize the complexity of public opinion in their report on a survey of Texans' attitudes about response to criminals. While the respondents expressed a desire for more prisons, they were equally in favor of simultaneous development of community corrections programs. In fact, Cullen, et al. (1985) suggest that "get tough" policies probably do reflect (or at least do not violate) public sentiments but decision makers seem to have missed the complexity of the public's views and failed to see and acceptance of rehabilitative and reform oriented policies as well.

Polls conducted by the University of South Carolina also found both punitive and rehabilitative attitudes held by their respondents. A primary factor in distinguishing which philosophy dominated was whether the offender was violent or nonviolent. While South Carolinians clearly wanted violent criminals behind bars, they just as decidedly favored such alternatives as community service, victim restitution, electronic surveillance, and closely-supervised probation for nonviolent offenders (College of Criminal Justice, 1986, 1987).

These studies imply that the general public is not as dogmatic about imprisonment for all criminals as we may have thought. However, since legislators and policy makers may be unaware of the potential for public support, pluralistic ignorance works to obstruct innovation in correctional and the development of options to imprisonment. One such potential area of innovation is an alternative known in the media as boot camp corrections. Before gauging public reaction to this program, its newness requires a description of its form and structure.

Boot Camp Corrections

In 1983, Georgia began a program called "shock incarceration" wherein a judge could sentence offenders (who agreed to participate) to a military style "boot camp" regimen under the direction of the Department of Corrections. The term "shock incarceration" is accurate (the program is located at a correctional facility and program failure may result in traditional prison assignment). However, it is also easily confused with the term "shock probation" which has been around a much longer time. Similar programs in other states have provided other names like Louisiana's IMPACT (Intensive Motivational Program of Alternative Correctional Treatment), and Regimented Inmate Discipline (RID) in Mississippi. The media has preferred the name "boot camp corrections" and, despite its informality, we choose to use it for its descriptive value.

Typical Programs

MacKenzie and Ballow (1989) identified eleven states operating boot camp programs. The oldest ones were those in Georgia (starting 1983), Oklahoma (1984) and Mississippi (1985). Florida, Louisiana, New York, and South Carolina began programs in 1987, while Alabama, Arizona, and Michigan followed in 1988. Texas' 1989 program offers a recent version. Current programs draw their participants primarily from impressionable, young adult felons who are not hardened criminals (General Accounting Office, 1988). For example, the New York program is limited to non-violent felony offenders age 16-24 and serving their first term in state prison (Schaefer, 1988).

The inmates are assigned to the program either by direct sentence from a judge (with inmate acceptance), or by corrections officials (with judicial approval), choosing from a list of volunteers from inmates originally sentenced to prison. The inmates spend anywhere from 90 to 180 days in the boot camp program at which time successful completion gains their placement on probation (typically at maximum supervision level) for the remainder of their sentence. Failure to complete either the program or probation may result in return to prison or to the judge for re-sentencing (General Accounting Office, 1988).

Program Structure

The typical boot camp program provides a highly regimented agenda involving strict discipline, drill and ceremony, and physical training. Most of the programs reviewed by the General Accounting Office (1988) require hard physical labor (e.g., clearing land, digging ditches, draining swamps) in addition to institution maintenance and housekeeping. While marching, shining shoes, and doing pushups, the inmates are learning discipline, self-esteem, determination, punctuality, cooperation, and attention to detail. They are, in other words, learning they can control their bodies, their tongues, and their actions (Rivers, n.d.).

A story reported by Rivers (n.d.) provides an inmate's perspective on the regimen's impact:

Yeah, yeah! The day we kept duck walking the fence. I couldn't do it. I just fell over. Then I remembered, I did it before so I must could do it again. So I duck walked some more. The guy behind me -- he fell down just before I did -- he said 'hey wait' and got up and started off again. I guess he figured if I didn't quit he wouldn't either (Rivers, n.d.).

While discipline and physical training/labor are key to all the programs, it is important to note that most also include activities in areas like education and counseling, community service, vocational assessment, job seeking skills, health education, drug and alcohol treatment.

Benefits of the program

Boot camp corrections has been proclaimed as filling both general correctional goals and more specific administrative aims. The correctional goals are an interesting combination of deterrence and rehabilitation/reintegration. For the former, it is assumed that the unpleasantness of the boot camp experience will make inmates want to avoid serving further time in prison (General Accounting Office, 1988; Staff, 1987). Or, as Flowers (1986) put it, a brief period of incarceration under harsh physical conditions, strenuous manual labor and exercise within a structured environment will "shock" the younger and less serious criminally oriented offender out of a future life of crime. The rehabilitation/re-integration objective is achieved when the boot camp experience enhances the inmate's capabilities for living a law-abiding life as a result of the self-control, self-esteem or educational experience gained from successful program completion (Flowers, 1986; General Accounting Office, 1988).

The programs are popular for administrative purposes since they may serve to (1) appease the public's perceived desire to "do something about crime" (Staff, 1987; Staff, 1988), (2) can serve to control prison crowding problems (Falcioni, 1988; Staff, 1987; Yurkanin, 1988), and (3) may reduce the costs associated with handling the inmate (Yurkanin, 1988). The cost aspect is, however, a potentially misleading argument. Florida, for example, spends $32.40 per day to house an inmate in prison with each inmate staying about four years. The cost to Florida for an inmate in a boot camp program increases to about $34.00 per day, but they will only stay 90 days (Falcioni, 1988). New York estimates that a camp operating for one year with 500 inmates will cost about $9,000 per inmate compared with a $19,400 cost under regular prison conditions (Yurkanin, 1988). A possibly hidden cost are expenses incurred by the probation department which must provide expensive supervision at the intensive or maximum level when the prisoner finisher boot camp.

Problems of the program

The problems associated so far with boot camp corrections tend to center on such concepts as discrimination, abuse, and net widening. Because participation in boot camp programs require a physically fit person, strict medical requirements typically restrict program eligibility to those capable of a high level of physical conditioning and work (Flowers, 1986). The potential for both physical and verbal abuse is also recognized. Oklahoma officials, for example, discovered they could not leave staff at the program for more than six months. After that time, they tended to over-exercise their authority (Pagel, 1986). Some have suggested that abuse is present in the form of dehumanizing effects which the strict regimen presents. But, as the Georgia A.C.L.U. chapter noted, it would be very difficult to get the courts to see as cruel and unusual something used daily by the military (Staff, 1988).

Net widening refers to the potential for a program designed as an alternative to incarceration to attract persons who would have actually received less supervision, rather than those for whom the program was designed. While boot camp may well reduce the number of persons placed in prison, this can only be done if the persons placed in the boot camp programs are ones who would have been sent to prison anyway. In other words, any net widening effect boot camps may have will offset potential lessening of the prison population. This would seem to be more likely in states where inmates are sentenced directly to the program by a judge (who might have placed the person on probation had the program not existed) than in states where boot camp participants are chosen from among those persons already sentenced to prison. In any event, it is a potential problem which must be considered as program evaluations are conducted.

Methodology

We became interested in the topic of boot camp corrections after hearing it discussed at the 1988 Annual Congress of the American Correctional Association. Speakers at a section devoted to these programs noted the paucity of either descriptive or evaluative information on this alternative to imprisonment. Of particular interest to us, however, were comments regarding the "marketing" of the program to the public. For example, Dale Parent (1988) noted that boot camp corrections had both punitive and rehabilitative aims but the former would be emphasized when presented to the public. About a month later, one of us was serving on a policy committee charged with developing guidelines for an Intensive Supervision Probation program initiated in the local judicial district. Despite what appeared to be obvious rehabilitative features (e.g., maintain a job and positive family relations, access to community services, avoiding the stigma of incarceration, etc.) the program was presented as an option to prison rather than an alternative to probation. The emphasis was on its punitive (e.g., house detention, electronic surveillance, mandatory drug testing, etc.) rather than rehabilitative aspects. The fact these two anecdotes actually reflected a "marketing plan" intrigued us. This encouraged a study to determine if the general public was emphatically opposed to correctional programs based on rehabilitative goals. Because the boot camp corrections programs included punitive features (e.g., strict discipline, physical training and labor) and less obvious rehabilitative ones (e.g., learning respect for authority, raising self-esteem), it was chosen as the specific program about which subjects would be asked.

A twelve question survey was given to 139 people in a variety of sites (e.g., hotels, offices, stores, homes, class rooms).

Because boot camp corrections is still an unfamiliar term, the questionnaire began with the following paragraph briefly defining such programs.

All across our country, states are trying to find ways to reduce prison overcrowding, prison costs, and the returning of persons to prison after their release. We would like to request your assistance in gauging public attitudes toward a new program for adult offenders which may help respond to those problems. The program is called "boot camp corrections" because, instead of going to a regular prison, the inmate is sentenced to a facility which provides a highly structured environment involving strict discipline, military drills, marching, and calisthenics. The boot camp lasts for 3 to 6 months (instead of a typical 2 to 3 year sentence) and upon successful completion of the program the inmate is returned to the community and placed on probation for the remainder of the sentence. Persons failing to complete the boot camp are sent to regular prison.

Subjects were then asked if they would support the use of such a program in their state (question #1) and what type criminal should be considered for that program (question #2). The choices for the second question were: non-violent, violent, first time offender, male, female, and repeat offender. Subjects were then told that regardless of their answer to question 2, they should respond to questions 3 and 4 as if only young, non-violent, first time, adult male offenders would be placed in the program. The intent was to encourage responses from subjects who may not be in favor of such a program but were in a position of living in a state where one was being implemented. Those characteristics reflect the type of inmate in existing boot camp programs. Question 3 then asked respondents which of three reasons would MOST encourage their support for the program if their state had decided to start one. The options (of which only one could be chosen) included:

a. The program reduces overcrowded prisons.

b. The program costs less than it would to put
    the same individual in prison.

c. The program helps inmates adjust to authority
    and become law-abiding citizens after their
    release.

Similarly, question 4 asked respondents which of three
aspects of the program would trouble them the most if
their state had decided to start a boot camp facility. The
options (of which only one could be chosen) included:

a. The inmates spend only 3 to 6 months in confine-
    ment instead of the regular term of imprisonment
    (for example, 3 years).

b. Persons who may have been placed on probation
    without any prison time may instead by put
    in "boot camp" and therefore receive more
    punishment than they would have otherwise.

c. The program is discriminatory since inmates
    with physical impairments cannot participate.

Questions five through eleven requested information about
the respondents' sex, education, age, occupation, military
history, military rank, and income.

An additional question asked them to mark on a scale (see
Figure 1) where they felt their opinions on crime and punishment would fall. They were not simply asked for their
political persuasion since it is possible for someone to consider themselves, for example, a political "liberal" yet
have very "conservative" views on how criminals should
be treated. Instead, we hoped to measure the respondents'
"punitive persuasion" as being either liberal, moderate,
or conservative. Allowing subjects to place themselves
on a continuum, rather than checking one of three seemingly

mutually exclusive categories, was intended to increase response level and subject comfort. Ninety-six percent (N=55), and the right third indicated conservative (N=49).

Figure 1

moderate

---

liberal   conservative

As the data are comprised primarily of nominal level measurement, responses were gathered as frequencies and subjected to cross tabulations and chi squared techniques. The non-random sample reflects a reasonably diverse population with 50% males (N=70) and 50% females (N=69) at all educational levels (except "less then 12 years"), ages (except under 18), and income brackets. Despite the presence of subjects in each age category, the 35-44 (N=16), 45=54 (N=5), 55-64 (N=3), and 65+ (N=3) were collapsed to one category of 35 and over (N=27) making it more similar to the remaining two categories of 18-24 (N=82) and 25-34 (N=30). In addition, the few subjects with military experience (N=17) required that we drop that variable from the cross tabulations.

Results

The idea of a boot camp corrections program received broad based support among the subjects with 78% replying that they would support the use of such a program in their state. The support does not vary by sex, age, education, occupation, income level or punitive persuasion. In other words, support for boot camp corrections was found among both males and females of all ages, occupations, educational and income levels, and regardless of whether the subjects saw themselves as having liberal, moderate, or conservative opinions on crime and punishment.

Figure 2   Reason for Supporting Boot Camp Corrections by Percent of
           Responses

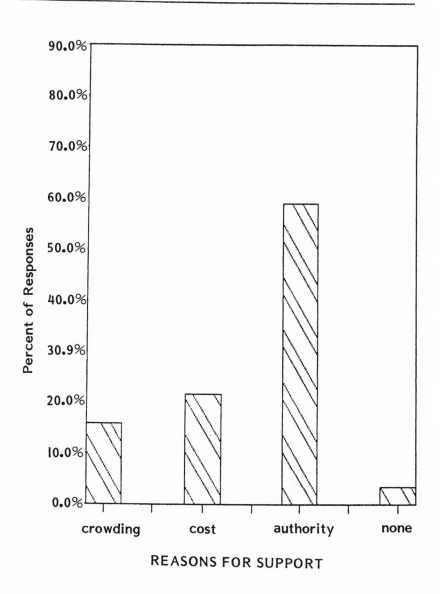

The majority of subjects (59%) were most likely to support boot camp corrections because of the program helping inmates adjust to authority and become law abiding citizens after their release (see Figure 2). The least support was given for boot camp corrections as a means of reducing overcrowded prisons (16%) or as simply a cost saving effort (22%). The choosing of one of those three responses was not influenced by the subject's sex, age, occupation, income, nor punitive persuasion. However, there was a greater tendency (not significant) for liberals age 18-24 to support the program because it would "help inmates adjust to authority" (70% of the young liberals indicated that reason) than it was for moderates (50%) and conservatives (57%). Thus, while a majority of respondents were attracted to the "adjust to authority" response, this was especially true for young liberals (see Table 1).

Table 1

Reasons for Supporting Boot Camp Corrections by Punitive Persuasion and Age

| | AGE 18-24 | | |
REASON	LIBERAL (n=20)	MOD (n=36)	CONSERVATIVE (n=21)
reduce crowding	15%	25%	5%
less cost	15%	17%	38%
adjust to authority	70%	58%	57%
Total	100%	100%	100% p < .15

AGE 25-34

REASON	LIBERAL (n=5)	MOD (n=7)	CONSERVATIVE (n=15)
reduce crowding	20%	0%	20%
less cost	20%	29%	13%
adjust to authority	60%	71%	67%
Total	100%	100%	100% p < .75

AGE 35 +

REASON	LIBERAL (n=4)	MOD (n=8)	CONSERVATIVE (n=13)
reduce crowding	25%	13%	15%
less cost	25%	0%	39%
adjust to authority	50%	88%	46%
Total	100%	101%	100% p < .35

The aspect of the program found most troubling to the subjects was that inmates in boot camp corrections would spend only three to six months in confinement instead of the regular term of imprisonment (see Figure 3). Seventy-one percent of the subjects were most troubled by that facet while 17% felt the program's discrimination against inmates with physical impairments was the more serious problem. Only 7% were concerned that persons placed in boot camp corrections may not have received any prison time at all if the program did not exist (e.e., net widening).

Figure 3   Troubling Aspects of Boot Camp Corrections by percent of
Responses

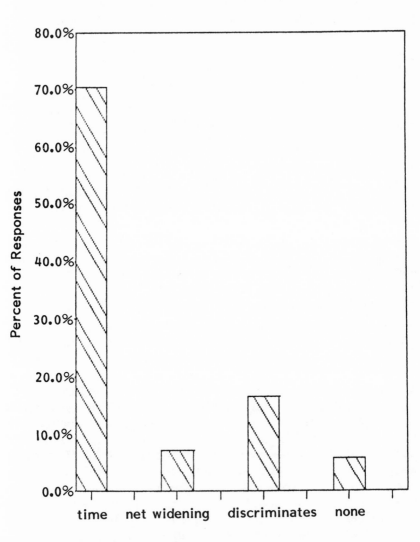

The specific choice among those three was not influenced by sex, age, occupation, or income. However, one's punitive persuasion did seem to make a difference (p < .01) with moderates and conservatives especially troubled by the less prison time feature (see Table 2). This was particularly true (p < .01) for young moderates and conservative (see Table 3).

Table 2

Troubling Aspects of Boot Camp Corrections
by Punitive Persuasion

REASON	LIBERAL (n=29)	MOD (n=51)	CONSERVATIVE (n=48)
less time	55%	77%	83%
net widening	3%	14%	4%
discriminates	41%	10%	13%
Total	99%	101%	100% p < .01

The subjects agreed that boot camp corrections would be most appropriately used for either male or female non-violent, first-time offenders. Of the 137 subjects responding to this question, anywhere from 108 to 124 chose those characteristics as suitable for inmates in the boot camp program. Far fewer chose either violent (31 responses) or repeat (36 responses) offenders as being proper (see Figure 4).

Table 3

Troubling Aspects of Boot Camp Corrections
by Punitive Persuasion and Age

	AGE 18-24		
REASON	LIBERAL (n=20)	MOD (n-36)	CONSERVATIVE (n=21)
less time	55%	81%	91%
net widening	5%	14%	0%
discriminates	40%	6%	10%
Total	100%	101%	101% p < .01

	AGE 25-34		
REASON	LIBERAL (n=5)	MOD (n=6)	CONSERVATIVE (n=14
less time	40%	67%	86%
net widening	0%	17%	0%
discriminates	60%	17%	14%
Total	100%	101%	100% p < .15

REASON	LIBERAL (n=4)	AGE 35 + MOD (n=9)	CONSERVATIVE (n=13)
less time	75%	67%	69%
net widening	0%	11%	15%
discriminates	25%	22%	15%
Total	100%	100%	99% p > .95

Figure 4   Types of Offenders Considered Appropriate for Boot Camp
Corrections by Percent of Responses

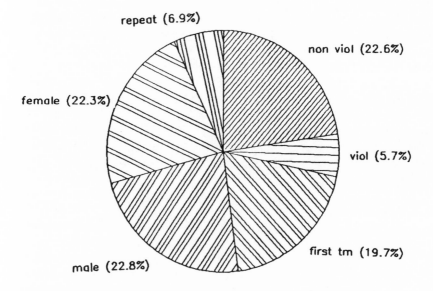

Conclusion

This study supports Gottfredson and Taylor's (1984) argument that public attitudes toward the criminal offender includes a utilitarian component (deterrence and rehabilitation) rather than a simple "knee-jerk" punitive one. However, like the South Carolina polls (College of Criminal Justice, 1986, 1987), those attitudes were more likely to be present when the offenders are non-violent rather than violent. As Cullen, et al. (1985) suggested, public sentiment regarding response to criminals is more complex than decision-makers seem to realize.

Since boot camp corrections combines both deterrent and rehabilitative objectives at the expense of long term incapacitation, it seemed an ideal program upon which to gauge public attitude. As the survey results show, the public is willing to support alternatives to imprisonment for both deterrent and rehabilitative resons. This is especially so if the inmates placed in the program are neither violent nor repeat offenders. The broad base of support shown by the sample further suggests that policy makers should willingly put forward creative alternatives to imprisonment and feel free to emphasize both the rehabilitative and punitive aspects.

Some correctional programs seem to be inherently attractive to persons of different punitive persuasions. Work release, for example, appeals to conservatives favoring the payment of room and board, restitution, and other fees by the offender as s/he learns the virtues of hard work. Those with a more liberal perspective emphasize the rehabilitative aspects gained from positive community and family contacts, self-reliance, and avoidance of the prison environment. Similarly, boot camp corrections has attraction for a wide cross-section of punitive persuasions. In its attempt to provide offenders with strict discipline and rigorous physical labor (deterrence), it tries to help them learn to adjust to authority, instill order and discipline in their lives, and become law-abiding citizens (rehabilitation). While this study found the rehabilitation aspect to be particularly intriguing to the "liberal" subjects, it was also important for half of the "moderates" and 43% of the "conservatives."

The finding of support for rehabilitation aspects becomes more important in light of recent research by Sechrest (1989) who provides a negative appraisal of boot camps, and correctly cautions against "gimmick" programs. He argues that shock incarceration is unlikely to be any more effective than scared straight or shock probation. The inclusion of education, job training, and skill development components may, however, warrant continued use of boot camp programs as a tool in the correctional arsenal (cf., Sechrest, 1989).

Our study suggests that the public is not against including components such as those in alternative to prison programs. Policy makers, legislators, and corrections officials need not hide behind strictly punitive objectives when talking to the public. A majority of persons (especially "moderates" and "conservatives") will be concerned about inmates spending less actual time in prison. However, if the program is used for either male or female, first-time non-violent offenders, the public reaction should be favorable. In addition, an explanation regarding the deterrent and rehabilitative features of the program will likely encourage broad-based support from the general public.

The suggestion by Gottfredson and Taylor (1984) that a situation of pluralistic ignorance is at work to stifle prison alternatives seems to be both appropriate and relevant. The assumption that "get tough on crime" means "put everyone in prison" perpetuates a myth, exacerbates the problem of prison crowding, and inhibits innovation. In an effort to avoid those problems, we agree with Riley and Rose (1980) in their call to increase responsiveness to public opinion by providing decision makers with empirical data using scientific survey techniques.

REFERENCES

College of Criminal Justice. 1986. **Fear of Crime Poll.** Columbia, SC: University of South Carolina.

College of Criminal Justice. 1987. **Fear of Crime Poll.** Columbia, SC: University of South Carolina.

Cullen, Francis T., Clark, Gregory A., and Wozniak, John F. 1985. Explaining the get tough movement: Can the public be blamed? **Federal Probation**, June, 16-24.

Falcioni, John G. 1988, May 9. Camps don't coddle cons, inmates get shock training. **Time.**

Flowers, Gerald T. 1986, March. **An Evaluation of the Use and Performance of Special Alternative Incarceration in Georgia.** (Available from: Georgia Department of Corrections, Office of Evaluation and Statistics, 2 MLK, Jr. Drive, Suite 870-B, Atlanta, GA 30334.

General Accounting Office. 1988. **Prison boot camps: Too early to measure effectiveness** (GOA/GGD-88-125Br). Washington, D.C.: United States General Accounting Office.

Gottfredson, Stephen, & Taylor, Ralph. 1984. Public policy and prison populations: Measuring opinions about reform. **Judicature, 68,** 190-201.

Immarigeon, Russ. 1986. Surveys reveal broad support for alternative sentencing. **Journal (The National Prison Project),** Fall, 1-4.

MacKenzie, Doris L. & Ballow, Deanna B. 1989. Shock incarceration programs in state correctional jurisdictions-An update. **NIJ Reports** (No. 214, May/June). Washington, D.C.: National Institute of Justice.

Pagel, Al. 1986, November. Doing a tour of duty in a 'boot camp' prison. **Corrections Compendium,** pp. 1, 8-11.

Parent, Dale. 1988. Boot camp corrections: Dare to discipline. American Correctional Association Annual Congress, Denver, CO.

Riley, P. J. & Rose, V. M. 1980. Public vs. elite opinion on correctional reform: Implications for social policy. **Journal of Criminal Justice, 8,** 345-356.

Rivers, Griffin H. (n.d.). **Boot Camp Bill.** (Available from National Institute on Corrections, Boulder, CO).

Schaefer, Steve. 1988, April. Press gets first look at Monterey shock camp. **Department of Correctional Services/Today** (New York), pp. 3-8.

Sechrest, Dale K. 1989. Prison "boot camps" do not measure up. **Federal Probation, 53** (3): 15-20.

Staff. 1987, October. Results of shock incarceration survey. **Association of State Correctional Administrators,** p. 8.

Staff. 1988, March 13. Shape up, son! **The Oregonian.** Yurkanin, Ann (1988, June). Trend toward shock incarceration increasing among states. **Corrections Today,** p. 87.

CHAPTER SEVEN

AMERICAN POLICING: A TIME FOR REORGANIZATION

William Nardini

In recent years more and more questions have been raised concerning the highly decentralized structure of policing in the United States. The organization of police agencies is essentially the same as it has been at the turn of the century resulting in far too many small independent police departments. Given the nature of our current society, such an archaic structure compromises police efficiency, not to mention the necessary duplication of personnel and equipment. The author recommends the consolidation of police agencies within our constitutional framework.

INTRODUCTION

The United States, since the turn of the century, has developed into a highly industrialized and urbanized society with a current population of some 230,000,000 people. The rapid growth of advanced technology and the mobility of the population have brought about a very complex and mass-oriented society to America. While private enterprise and some units of government have restructured to more adequately meet the needs of current America, the basic organizational structure of law enforcement is fundamentally the same as it was in the early part of this century.

There are in the United States approximately 757,508 police personnel who work in approximately 15,000 state and local agencies (Bureau of Justice Statistics, 1989). The vast majority of these personnel work in separate and small county, city, town, or suburban police agencies. Each is an entity onto itself with separate police administrators, facilities, jurisdiction and line personnel. Each police agency, with few exceptions, is under the control of a separate governmental unit. This leads to a costly duplication of function and resources, and often results in the lack of a well-coordinated and efficient performance of police service. This is an anachronism and cannot, in 1990, be justified on the basis of our constitutional form of government, an argument one suspects is most often used by local politicians who wish to retain control of the police service. In the early years of this nation, such a police structure was justified given the limited means of communication, transportation, and the low population density and mobility. Presently, however, a restructuring and consolidation of police agencies in this country is long overdue.

Current Police Organization

In the United States, at the federal level, there are approximately 50 separate law enforcement agencies with a total of 61,342 police personnel (Sourcebook, 1987). The major federal agencies include the Federal Bureau of Investigation, the Drug Enforcement Administration, the U.S. Marshals Service and the Immigration and Naturalization Service all within the Department of Justice, as well as the U.S. Customs Service, the Internal Revenue Service, the Secret Service and the Bureau of Alcohol, Tobacco, and Firearms as a part of the Treasury Department. Additionally, there are other investigative units in sundry Federal agencies. During the twentieth century, the changing nature of our society with its modern methods of communication and transportation as well as passage of an increasing number of federal laws has greatly expanded the law enforcement responsibilities of federal agencies. Over the years the unsystematic growth of federal agencies has produced a fragmentation of federal police powers, an overlapping of jurisdiction and a confusion and rivalry that have interfered with administrative efficiency (Caldwell and Nardini, 1977).

An even more serious problem exists at the local level where the vast majority of police personnel and agencies are located. Of the 737,741 police personnel in this country, 568,743 are at the county, municipal and local levels. Of the 40,000 separate police agencies, approximately 39,750 are county, municipal or other local governmental units each with its separate police department. Most noteworthy is the fact that these agencies have 79% of all police personnel and most of these agencies have fewer than 50 police officers (Sourcebook, 1987). Stated differently, there are over 50 state police agencies, about 3,043 counties each with their own sheriff's police, 17,977 municipalities, 17,149 township governments and 18,323 special districts and all of these separate governmental units, with few exceptions, have their own police force. This country has a highly fragmented police and criminal justice system resulting from the large number of uncoordinated local governments and law enforcement agencies.

Concomitant with the number and fragmented nature of police organizations, is the number, quality, method of appointment and tenure of police administrators in the United States. At the federal level each enforcement agency has its own administrative director and staff, as well as agency autonomy and resources.

At the state level, the chief law enforcement administrator is appointed by the governor and serves at the pleasure of the governor. There are minimal educational requirements and usually the administrator is required to have had experience in police work. Such appointments are made from within the state police agency itself. Recommended improvements in the qualifications and appointment procedure will be discussed later in this article. Since this writer is advocating a statewide police system, the only criticism of the current state policing structure and administration deals with administrative qualifications and lack of job tenure. Additionally, the organizational structure of state police agencies will have to be modified to assume the responsibility for total law enforcement throughout the individual states.

It is at the county, municipal, and local levels of policing that the most significant administrative and organizational changes are required to best perform the policing function in 1990 America. Administratively we find thousands of mostly small autonomous police agencies each with its own chief administrator, support staff and resources.

At the county level of government, and with few exceptions, we have the only politically elected police administrator called the sheriff. This position was developed from the early English system which was abandoned in England years ago, but which we continue to retain because of the constitutional nature of the office and the power of local political interests. There are no professional qualifications or experience requirements, and all that is required is for one to get elected. How truly absurd in this day an age! Almost all of the more than 3,000 counties in the U.S. has an elected sheriff, a separate jail, its own deputy sheriffs, and their separate resources. Throughout each state there is the duplication of services, resources and administrative and field personnel. To illustrate, the state police often have state wide jurisdiction and the county, city, and local police all perform services within a single county, but yet are independent police departments. How archaic, anachronistic, inefficient and what a waste of the taxpayer's money.

In cities, suburbs, and small towns throughout the country we have chiefs of police for each department who are usually appointed by politicians and serve at the pleasure of the chief political executive. Mandatory educational qualifications are usually minimal and such police administrators can be removed at the discretion of the political executive. In fact the average tenure of a chief of police is usually 3-5 years with the result being a lack of administrative and organizational stability and low morale of personnel. In essence, law enforcement is highly decentralized and suffers from needless duplication of efforts, overlapping of jurisdiction, lack of coordination, and the redundancy of services and resources. Interagency cooperation is insufficient. What is necessary is the consolidation of police agencies (Caldwell & Nardini, 1977).

RECOMMENDED POLICE REORGANIZATION

At the Federal level of government, all criminal law enforcement personnel should be consolidated into a single
bureau of law enforcement, or other appropriate organizational entity, to be located within the Department of Justice.
Such a bureau would have a chief administrator appointed
for a term of 10 years and could be removed only for cause.
The Bureau of Law Enforcement would be responsible for
all Federal criminal law enforcement, and thus all existing
enforcement agencies would be consolidated. This would
eliminate the unnecessary duplication of function and resources, and allow for a more efficient, effective and well--
coordinated enforcement effort. The domestic intelligence
function should be removed from the F.B.I. and transferred
to the C.I.A. given the distinct nature of the intelligence
role and its close relationship to foreign intelligence.

Perhaps the most significant and important police reorganization should occur at the state and local level of government.
All existing and separate county, city, suburb or town law
enforcement agencies would be merged into a single statewide law enforcement agency or department. In essence,
each state will have a single statewide police structure,
with a chief law enforcement administrator, responsible
for all law enforcement functions within a respective state.
Thus, there would be 50 state police agencies, and a single
federal law enforcement organization. The positions of
sheriff and town marshal should be abolished and each
state should be divided into police districts without regard
to county, city or town boundaries. There currently exists
a state police agency in every state except Hawaii, and
consolidation of local police personnel would not be difficult.

THE APPOINTMENT OF POLICE ADMINISTRATORS

All of the top administrators of the federal and state police
agencies described above would be appointed on the basis
of education, law enforcement experience, and merit and

would be selected by nonpartisan nominating commissions at the federal and state level similar to the "Missouri Plan" for the selection of judges as recommended by the National Advisory Commission on Criminal Justice Standards and Goals, 1973. Chief police administrators would be appointed for a term of 10 years, to overlap political administrations, and removal would only be for cause. These administrators would be required to have a college degree in criminology, criminal justice, or law, and have an appropriate amount of line and supervisory police experience. This writer disagrees with the current practice of appointing a judge as Director of the F.B.I. given the highly educated, experienced and qualified number of bureau personnel suitable for such a promotion, and the fact that most judges are not experienced in law enforcement.

CONCLUDING COMMENTS

The reorganization of American police agencies is necessary to more effectively perform a vital governmental service by eliminating overlapping jurisdictions, the costly duplication of services, inefficient operations, jurisdictional disputes and a myriad of other problems. Small agencies usually lack adequate resources to provide total police services, and criminal mobility is no longer a local problem but a statewide and interstate problem. As a result, law enforcement has been hampered in its ability to respond effectively (Police, 1973). Consolidation is essential. Local government is incapable of adequately meeting the total crime problem. Our current fragmentation of police services results because of the large number of uncoordinated local law enforcement agencies. Although law enforcement officials speak of close cooperation between agencies, such is often informal, ineffective and inadequate to meet the needs of a modern, technologically advanced and highly urban nation. Even if cooperation was excellent it is not enough. The lack of a coordinated administrative and organizational structure, as well as standardized procedures, often creates confusion and renders police efforts fruitless (Nardini & Caldwell, 1977).

The argument that the centralization of law enforcement at the state level threatens our constitutional form of government is nonsense.

The federal system will remain with a separate federal and state police systems. It is not recommended that a single federal police agency be established for the entire country. This nation is too large and complex for such a structure, and it could threaten our form of government even though such has not occurred in recent history in any of the western democracies having a single centralized police structure. Along with the consolidation of police agencies there should be a similar restructuring of the remaining parts of the criminal justice system, i.e., the courts, prosecution and corrections. Much has already been done at the appellate court level. States have always administered correctional institutions, parole, and in many instances probation. A major overhaul of the prosecutorial function is needed.

An important reason for the recommended change in the appointment and retention of chief law enforcement administrators is to establish a stable, highly educated and experienced personnel who would have job security to perform professionally, and to remove them from the control of political executives. There is no greater negative influence on effective and professional law enforcement than that resulting from political interference and control. It is about time that this great nation organizationally and administratively modernize a critical governmental service.

REFERENCES

Bureau of Justice Statistics. 1989. Profile of State and Local Law Enforcement Agencies, 1987. Washington, D.C.: U.S. Department of Justice.

Caudwell, Robert G., and Nardini, William. 1977. Foundations of law enforcement and criminal justice. Indianapolis, IN: Bobbs-Merrill.

National advisory commission on criminal justice standards and goals: Police, 1973. Washington, D.C.: U.S. GPO.

The President's Commission on law enforcement and administration of justice: Task Force Report: The Police. 1967. Washington, D.C.: U.S. GPO.

United States Department of Justice, Bureau of Justice Statistics: Sourcebook of Criminal Justice Statistics, 1987. Washington, D.C.: GPO.

CHAPTER EIGHT

TEACHING ETHICS IN CRIMINAL JUSTICE

David P. Schmidt

and

Joseph L. Victor

This paper advances a number of practical suggestions for teaching ethics in college courses on criminal justice, which derive from the authors' experience in teaching and consulting. Thoughts are organized under 3 topics: (1) the process of teaching ethics, (2) the content of teaching ethics, and (3) the questions of indoctrination.

The focus on courses in criminal justice, warranted by the authors' expertise in this area, is further justified by the acute ethical dilemmas that arise in the criminal justice system.

INTRODUCTION

The ethical misconduct of leaders in all segments of society is stimulating renewed interest in ethics education. If there is a growing consensus that ethics should permeate the learning process, there still are many practical questions about how to teach ethics in courses that do not focus specifically on the subject of ethics. Thus many approaches are being developed to teach ethics in medicine, business, journalism, public policy and other subjects.

This article advances several practical suggestions for teaching ethics in college courses on criminal justice, which stem from our experience in teaching and consulting. Our thoughts will be organized under three topics: (1) The process of teaching ethics, (2) The content of teaching ethics, and (3) The question of indoctrination.

Our focus on courses in criminal justice, which is warranted by our expertise in this area, is further justified by the acute ethical dilemmas that arise in the criminal justice system. According to P. E. Murphy (1983):

> There is no area, perhaps, in which ethical dilemmas are more prominently seen and their mishandling more forcefully placed before the public eye than the Criminal Justice System. Morally enigmatic choices continually challenge the personnel on all operational and managerial levels of the system's three major branches: the police, the courts, and corrections (p. 1).

We would note, however, that our suggestions for teaching ethics in courses on criminal justice are pertinent to teaching ethics in courses on other substantive topics.

The Process of Teaching Ethics

The process of teaching is of critical importance for subjects that raise questions of ethics. **How** we teach ethics in criminal justice courses is informed by the characteristics of students that we typically encounter and by our assumptions about the objectives of college level education.

We feel that the students whom we teach should be viewed as prospective criminal justice agents. Their outlook is active, not passive, and emphatically pragmatic. Many of our students have extensive work experience and bring to the classroom a business-like orientation to problem solving. Their interest lies primarily in solving applied issues, not in theoretical or metaethical analysis. Accordingly, it is important to raise ethics issues in ways that speak meaningfully to the particular concerns that arise from the experiences of these students.

How we teach ethics also rests upon two closely related assumptions we have about the objectives of a college education. The first assumption is that college students should be challenged to learn how to learn. Though mastery of foundational materials is absolutely necessary, the primary objective of college education is not merely to have students memorize facts. College students should acquire an independent facility in researching and thinking about the information that they are studying. Rogers (1983) maintained that the educated person is one who understands the provisional nature of knowledge and who finds security in the ongoing process of seeking new knowledge. This commitment to continual adaptation through the accumulation of new knowledge should be the hallmark of college education.

Our second assumption is that argumentation about interpretations is the distinctive mode of speech that characterizes college-level discourse. No longer should students passively digest accounts of the world: In college, they should develop the difficult but necessary skills of critical analysis and careful reasoning about different, sometimes conflicting accounts of reality. Or, as the Victorian education reformer John Robert Seeley (1971) said of the study of history:

> In history, everything depends upon turning narrative into problems.... Break the drowsy spell of narrative; ask yourself questions; set yourself problems; you will become an investigator; you will cease to be solemn and begin to be serious. (p. 139.)

Seeley's account about history applies to other fields as well, including criminal justice.

We have identified three ways to teach ethics that honor these assumptions about the student and college education. These interrelated processes are: (1) Mutual learning, (2) Cooperation on solving problems, and (3) Keeping a journal.

First to consider is the importance of mutual learning. The lecture method is an important and especially in some subjects, efficient means for presenting course material. However, the study of ethical issues in criminal justice calls for an approach that emphasizes mutual learning and dialogue among persons who have different expertise and who bring distinctive perspectives to the issues. Concerning the development of ethics in business, Charles McCoy (1985) says:

> In order to develop corporate ethics effectively, it is necessary to utilize diverse resources. Some of these resources are to be found among academics and from specialized resources. Other resources must come from the experience of persons actually working in societal, organizational contexts.... The development of corporate ethics depends on having this spectrum of persons not only present but also committed to the project and involved with one another. Each person and group has a crucial part of the whole--but still only a part. For these parts to interact fruitfully, there must be mutual learning and mutually interrelated inquiry. (pp. 89-90.)

In criminal justice courses, it can be very helpful to combine the academic insights of the instructor with the practical knowledge of persons with careers in criminal justice. If the criminal justice instructor is not formally trained in ethics, it may be helpful to invite an ethicist to participate in the dialogue in class.

However, merely bringing together people with these backgrounds and competences does not guarantee effective teaching about ethics in criminal justice. The kinds of people we have just described often lack a common language for discussing the ethics of criminal justice issues. Genuine dialogue depends on all participants' being willing to develop a process of mutual learning. Thus the effective criminal justice instructor must have the skills to facilitate a constructive dialogue among the conversation partners.

The best means for promoting mutual learning on ethics in criminal justice is to have students listen to and participate in conversations with criminal justice professionals, ethicists and other appropriate persons. We have tried inviting people to speak in class or to address larger groups of students in special conferences or auditorium presentations. Video-taped presentations can also be used, although the best format is one that allows conversational interaction. Other means for encouraging active mutual learning among students include role-playing, simulation games, reading aloud from novels and plays, and student presentations.

Second to consider is the importance of cooperation on solving problems. A helpful tool for teaching ethics is to have students work in pairs on solving problems. A recent article by A. Kohn, "It's Hard to Get Left Out of a Pair," (1987), supports the cooperative approach to learning. To support his assertion that people learn more through cooperation than competition, Kohn cites the example of two brothers who collaborated on an enormously successful professional career in education. Through their research on cooperation that encompasses eighty studies, these brothers concluded that students who learn cooperatively--compared with students who learn competitively or independently--learn better, feel better about themselves, and get along better with each other.

The cooperative approach to education requires students to work together, to communicate and to listen to one another on a regular basis. This approach stimulates them to take responsibility for their own learning as well as that of their fellow students. If one of the goals of education is to enable students to achieve some measure of autonomy and independence in their thinking, a powerful way to achieve this goal is through caring, supportive relationships and friendships, among students and between students and their teachers.

Thus many of our classroom exercises consist of separating the students into pairs to discuss an ethics case or to develop a joint presentation to bring back to the entire class. This supportive process provides a nonthreatening way for students to try out their ideas with each other, to verbalize together their new knowledge, to turn ideas over in their minds and to examine arguments critically from various perspectives. The enthusiastic response of many students to this interpersonal process of learning validates our commitment to cooperation in learning. One student's response is typical:

I find the teaching methods both relaxed and open. I think this is very important in a learning atmosphere. The fact we have a small class adds a feeling of safety. It's like meeting with friends instead of the usual classroom situation. The discussions we get going are great! They are especially useful to me.

A third process for teaching ethics is to have students keep journals as part of the criminal justice course. We have asked students to keep two journals: one for reflecting on class discussion and another for making notes about their assigned readings. They are to make notes on the right-hand pages of their journals and on the left-hand pages they are to record questions, conversations with other students, and open-ended questions. The students are encouraged to write about ethical concerns or issues that arise in class or in their readings. Throughout the course, these journals serve as a basis for individual conferences between the teacher and the student.

Having students keep a journal poses several significant challenges. Many students are uncomfortable, at least initially, with the open-ended nature of this assignment. Too many students today have never been challenged to do the independent and critical thinking that journals require. Second, reading and responding to a large number of journals places a significant burden on the teacher, not only in terms of the time that is required but also in terms of the expertise that this process calls for. The teacher must respond critically yet supportively to the insights and questions that students record in their journals. These challenges notwithstanding, keeping a journal helps students to probe deeply their developing ideas about ethical issues connected with the topics covered in criminal justice.

The Content of Teaching Ethics

In addition to the procedural question of **how** to teach ethics in criminal justice courses, there is the substantive question of **what** should be taught. While the specific answer to this question depends in large measure on the content of the particular course, there are some general points to be made about the content of any course that raises ethical issues. We believe that the conventional approach to applied ethics rests on a flawed paradigm that "applies" normative ethical theories to cases. We will note our objections to this conventional approach and offer an alternative approach to teaching ethics in courses on criminal justice.

The conventional approach to applied ethics presents ethical theories which are then applied to concrete cases. In many college books on applied ethics, this approach proceeds as follows: First there is a section in the book that develops the traditional normative theories of deontological ethics, teleological ethics, and theories of rights or justice. These theories are usually presented in terms of their development in the history of philosophy, which may be quite unrelated to the substantive topics and practices of the course on criminal justice. Then this book typically will have a section in which the theories are "applied" to actual cases in criminal justice.

We believe this conventional approach is flawed for three reasons. First, the presentation of the theories tends to be highly abstract and, to the student, irrelevant to the practical contexts that define the ethical issues that arise in criminal justice. Our experience is that students hurry through the "philosophical" portion of applied ethics textbooks in order to get to the "more interesting" case discussions. We do not believe that ethical theory is without value. We do believe that this way of presenting ethical theory, in its traditional philosophical garb and abstracted from actual cases, makes it difficult to demonstrate the relevance of theory.

A second problem with the conventional approach to applied ethics is that the application of theories to cases does not modify, challenge or strengthen the theories. The theories tend to remain abstracted and isolated from the insights and often valuable ethical points that students raise in relation to actual experiences and practices of criminal justice. This aloofness of theory from practice violates our commitment to mutual learning in the teaching of ethics. Ethical theory is helpful to the extent that it enters the conversation and becomes one voice among many. The outcome of mutual learning between theory and practice may be the **revision** of theories, an outcome opposed by the conventional approach to applied ethics.

Third, we doubt that theory alone can help students make ethical judgments about actual cases. Ethical theory purports to bring "clarity" to ethical experience and to apply analytical "rigor" to the task of sorting out ethical alternatives. But this analytical function does not help students decide what they **should do**. As Alasdair MacIntyre (1988) argues, theory only helps to sharpen the interminable differences between rival ethical stances. He says:

> Modern academic philosophy turns out by and large to provide means for a more accurate and informed definition of disagreement rather than for progress toward its resolution. Professors of philosophy who concern themselves with questions of justice and of practical rationality turn out to disagree with each other as sharply, as variously, and, so it seems, as irremediably upon how such questions are to be answered as anyone else (p. 3).

If the purpose of teaching ethics is to help students make ethical decisions for themselves, it is necessary to give them more than a philosophical awareness of theoretical disputes. We will now propose, as an alternative to the conventional approach to applied ethics, the teaching of argumentation in ethics.

We feel it is important to teach students that rational debate and arguments on ethics **is possible.** We need to show students that they can mount effective ethical arguments. The most frustrating response to an ethical issue is the student's plaintive, "Who's to say?" Students who ask this question are merely echoing the widespread tendency in our society to make ethics a matter of individual, undefendable opinion. We oppose this general skepticism about ethical claims. We seek to rid our students of this pernicious attitude. The best way to do this is to teach students the basic skills in constructing sound arguments on ethical issues. Among the many books on informal logic and practical reasoning, we have found particularly helpful for this purpose is **An Introduction to Reasoning** by Stephen Toulmin (1984). This book provides a candid map of an argument's construction that students can follow easily. It empowers them to develop sound, effective arguments for expressing and testing their ethical convictions on actual issues in criminal justice.

Making argumentation central to teaching ethics places us squarely in the "good reasons" school of ethical theory. This emphasis in ethics, which was popularized by Kai Nielsen (1958, 1959) and other philosophers, represents an intentional move away from the traditional metaethical question of "What is the good?" to the more practical question of "When is a reason a **good** reason for an ethical judgment?" In our work with students on ethics in criminal justice, we find that this "good reasons" approach to ethics helps students get at the ethical dimension of their subject. Theory can make a contribution at the level of sharpening students' arguments. For example, a student who is giving a cost-benefit argument for restricting the appeals process in the courts might find it useful to see that the argument is teleological in nature. At this point, ethical theory can support the student's ethics education. Making arguments, not theories, central to what is taught actually permits ethical theory to make a more helpful contribution to learning.

The Question of Indoctrination

A common objection to teaching ethics at the college level is that it is too late at this advanced stage in students' moral development to shape significantly their ethical outlook. According to this view, effective ethics education must occur at a much earlier age. It is ironic, therefore, that ethics education in college also encounters the charge of indoctrination--a charge that presumes it is still possible to affect the moral thinking and values of students even at the college level. While ethics education and training at early ages is very important and undoubtedly has a lasting impact on a person's moral character, we think that moral development is a life-long process. Accordingly, it is fair to presume that ethics education at the college level **can** shape students' substantive values and processes of moral reasoning. It is therefore imperative to consider whether and in what ways indoctrination poses a problem for teaching ethics in criminal justice courses.

First it is necessary to specify what we mean by indoctrination. A report from the Hastings Center (1980) defines indoctrination as a systematic attempt to persuade students of the validity of a belief system, one that (a) radically rules out the possibility of accepting other belief systems; (b) in a deliberate fashion, invokes withholding from students either serious objections to that system or those tools of analysis that would enable the student to see its flaws; (c) excludes the possibility of rejection of the belief system; and (d) penalizes deviation. The central element in this account of indoctrination is the denial of independent and critical thinking in ethics education.

The prohibition against teaching in a way that constitutes this form of indoctrination is warranted by the ethical duty at least not to thwart the development of independent moral agents. Furthermore, the requirements of the university prohibit us from indoctrinating our students. Ethicist Ronald Green (1989) summarizes the implications for indoctrination that stem from teaching in the university:

> I feel we have a primary loyalty as teachers within the university to the standards of the university itself, and those standards to me are the standards of critical inquiry, rational discourse, the communication (but the critical communication) of culture. Above all personal or private agendas for social transformation or ethical reform, our foremost responsibility has to be duty to our university context, to its traditions, and to our peers (p. 233).

We feel strongly that we should not dictate to students what they ought to think on particular issues in criminal justice. Our commitment to critical argumentation, and the approach we take on mutual learning, precludes our deciding in advance for students what they should think about any particular cases. As a matter of principle, this conviction seems to us to be unassailable. As a practical matter, however, it is difficult to know whether and when to make known in class our views on ethics issues. Students usually are curious about what we think on this or that issue. At the same time, before their minds are made up on an issue, students are easily swayed by the convictions of their instructor.

Our practice is to argue for our own views on an issue only after students have been allowed to develop their own views to a significant degree. And even then, we do so provisionally, subject to the canons of responsible and civil argumentation. One important point of teaching ethics: The instructor must always be ready to retract or modify an argument when confronted with convincing counter-argu-ments or rebuttals from the students. Only then do we, as teachers, validate our commitment to mutual learning and civility in argumentation.

While we do not indoctrinate on particular issues (i.e., whether **this** case constitutes corruption in a criminal justice agency), we do intentionally advocate general virtues and principles that are necessary for the possibility of doing ethics. In our words and especially in our deeds, we want to convince students that they should be honest (straightforward, nondevious), humane (sympathetic, not cruel) and just (fair, equitable, even-handed). Making these virtues and principles a condition for doing ethics is not unjustifiable moral indoctrination. Rather, it is necessary for students to have these basic convictions if they are to be able to debate particular issues at all. Edmund L. Pincoffs (1986) takes this view, saying:

> No one is a moral indoctrinator, then, because he inculcates in his pupil a distaste for dishonesty, a revulsion against cruelty, or a sense of outrage at injustice. In teaching his pupil in such a way as to encourage these **qualities of character**, he is not closing his pupil's mind, stunting his growth, or making it impossible for him to think for himself. He is, rather, giving him the **kind of character** without which he would be unable to carry on a moral discussion (p. 147).

We think that the commitment to critical inquiry in ethics education too often means that "anything goes, whatsoever." For the sake of ethics, this cannot be so. Thus while we do not indoctrinate on particular issues, we do seek to plant in our students a basic orientation toward good over evil.

Summary

These three topics--the process of teaching ethics, the content of teaching ethics, and the question of indoctrination--do not cover everything that might be said about teaching ethics in courses on criminal justice. We feel, however, that these topics constitute the most important considerations that should put to the growing array of innovations in teaching ethics.

REFERENCES

Green, Ronald. "The Ethics of Teaching Ethics: A Round Table Discussion." **The Annual of the Society of Christian Ethics, 1989.** Washington D.C.: Georgetown University Press, 1989, 233-254.

Hastings Center. **The Teaching of Ethics in Higher Education.** Hastings-on-Hudson, New York.: The Hastings Center, 1980, 59.

Kohn, A. "It's Hard to Get Left Out of a Pair." **Psychology Today.** October 1987, 53-57.

McCoy, Charles. **Management of Values: The Ethical Difference in Corporate Policy and Performance.** Boston: Pitman Publishing Inc., 1985.

MacIntyre, Alasdair. **Whose Justice? Which Rationality?** Notre Dame: University of Notre Dame Press, 1988.

Murphy, P. E. **The Teaching of Applied and Professional Ethics.** Paper presented at the annual meeting of the Criminal Justice Educators Association of New York State, Lake Placid, New York, April 1983.

Nielsen, Kai. "The 'Good Reasons Approach' and 'Ontological Justifications of Morality." **The Philosophical Quarterly.** April 1959, 116-130.

_____. "Good Reasons in Ethics: An Examination of the Toulmin-Hare Controversy." **Theoria** vol. 24, 1958, 11-26.

Pincoffs, Edmund L. **Quandaries and Virtues.** Lawrence, Kansas: University Press of Kansas, 1986.

Rogers, C. **Freedom to Learn for the 80's.** Columbus, Ohio: Charles E. Merrill, 1983.

Seeley, John Robert. **The Expansion of England.** Ed. by J. Gross. Chicago: University of Chicago Press, 1971.

Toulmin, Stephen, Richard Rieke, and Allan Janik. **An Introduction to Reasoning.** 2nd edition. New York: Macmillan Publishing Co., Inc., 1984.

CHAPTER NINE

TRENDS IN PROBATION AND PAROLE
EMPLOYEE UNIONIZATION

J. D. Jamieson

and

Barry D. Smith

Probation and parole officers are opting for unionization at higher rates than most public sector employees. In 1972, three probation and parole agencies were unionized. By 1981, nineteen probation and parole agencies were unionized. The current longitudinal study shows thirty-six probation and parole agencies unionized. The increase in probation and parole unionization has occurred despite an overall decrease in public sector unionization. The current study also assesses probation and parole administrators' perceptions regarding the influence of unionization on cost, difficulty of administration, and quality of services. Finally, the study examines union influence on areas such as hiring and termination, caseload size, promotion, in-service training, and agency policies.

INTRODUCTION

It is interesting, and perhaps surprising, to note that public sector employees belong to collective bargaining organizations at much higher rates than employees in the private sector. While union activity is generally associated with the giant labor unions in heavy industry and commerce, only 20% of the private sector employees in the United States belong to unions. Employees in the public sector,

those persons on federal, state, and local government pay-
rolls, are unionized at rates of 40-50% (Levin, et al., 1986).
There have been fluctuations in these percentages over
the years, including relatively rapid unionization of public
sector employees during the 1960s and 1970s, and then
a deceleration and declining trend during the 1980s.

The factors that influence the attractiveness of unions
to public sector employees are also interesting. Johnson
and Smith (1981) surmised that during the 1960s, the tendency
of public sector employees to unionize was facilitated
by the general acceptance of the idea that all citizens
had the right to inspect, question, and perhaps protest
existing government practices (Johnson and Smith, 1981).
This questioning naturally extended to parity issues between
public and private sector salaries, benefits, and working
conditions. Where public sector compensation was found
to be subpar, which was not at all rare, the collective bargaining power and political influence offered by organized
unions became naturally attractive. Johnson and Smith
further surmised that the union leadership recognized the
potential for organizing the public sector and aggressively
courted public sector employees. These factors, coupled
with the rapid growth in the size of the public sector work
force during this period, resulted in the high numbers, and
ratios of unionized public employees. By 1975, 50% of
all public employees were unionized, and the courts had
generally backed the unions when issues rose concerning
the legality and constitutionality of unionizing the public
sector (Shafritz, 1986).

During the late 1970s and through the 1980s, there has
been a decline in the unionization tendencies for public
sector employees in general (Lipset, 1986). Economic auster-
ity measures demanded by the public, such as Proposition
13, have caused state and local governments to reduce
spending. Tight budgets, forced personnel reductions for
lack of funds, and the general inability of state and local
governments to increase wages and benefits have apparently
reduced the attractiveness of unions to employees in the

public sector. Overall union membership in the public sector has thus been in decline, and with this decline has come a decrease in the political influence that made the unions attractive in the 1960s and 1970s. Also, legislation during the 1980s in some areas has allowed severe penalties for public employee strikes and other employee dispute actions. Some unions were either disbanded or were forced to make major job related concessions (Goldfield, 1987). Surviving public sector unions are finding that management has become more sophisticated in bargaining and other labor areas. In the Criminal Justice System the trend toward decreasing unionization for public employees has not always applied. Indeed, recent figures show that unions for police and correctional employees are still growing (Cole, 1985). Union activity among criminal justice employees, particularly the police and corrections officers, has been a sensitive issue because public safety may be jeopardized when a strike occurs. With the support of the courts, however, the police have remained heavily unionized, and trends indicate increases in union activity in some other justice related occupations.

THE CRIMINAL JUSTICE SYSTEM WORKFORCE

As reported in the 1981 Johnson and Smith article, the National Manpower Survey of the Criminal justice System projected that employment in state and local criminal justice agencies would increase from 916,000 in 1975 to 1,207,000 in 1985 (Department of Justice, 1978). Included in this projection were increases in police from 539,000 to 718,00; judicial workforce from 118,000 to 182,000; prosecution and legal employees from 45,000 to 79,000; and corrections personnel from 203,000 to 324,000. The 1986 Sourcebook of Criminal Justice statistics indicated that as of October 31, 1985, when this research began, there were 1,260,340 employees in state and local criminal justice agencies. Police employment reached 631,903; judicial employment rose to 165,903; prosecution and legal to 73,833; and correctional employment climbed to 372,761.

While all areas of the criminal justice system evidenced growth, only the area of corrections surpassed the projected increase (Department of Justice).

The growth in corrections is partially explained by the continuing increase in prison populations. From 1977-1987 prison populations increased from approximately 250,000 to 545,600 and continue to increase. The number of probationers rose from 775,820 to 2,094,405 (Department of Justice, 1987). These figures may be explained in part by the growing intolerance of crime and criminals by the American public. The "just desserts" philosophy of the 70s and 80s is well documented. Society is demanding a tough approach to crime and criminals, reduced government and lower taxes, and the Criminal Justice System is caught in between. Local and state governments are having to redistribute scarce resources. In the area of probation and parole, for example, full-time equivalent employees increased from 16,877 in 1967 to 29,681 in 1987 (Contact Center, 1987). At the same time, however, average caseloads for line personnel increased to unmanageable levels in some areas.

Historically, the police have had the most controversial role in the unionization of criminal justice employees. Line level police employees have always far outnumbered line level employees in other sections of the Criminal Justice System, and the issues surrounding collective bargaining by police have been the most sensitive from the public point of view. While the police were among the last to gain legislative and judicial approval to form bargaining unions, by 1978 over 60% of the police officers were working under collective bargaining contracts, and over half of the states had consented legislatively to police bargaining rights (Cole, 1985).

Unionization in the institutional corrections area was less sensitive than police unionization because of the smaller number of persons involved and the relative isolation of correctional officers from the public eye. However, unionization was resisted to a certain degree by correctional administrators who relied on autocratic management styles, and saw union influence in decision making as a threat to their ability to manage effectively. By 1980, however, there were 27 state correctional systems operating under negotiated union contacts, and others with active employee organizations (Smith and Sapp, 1985). The unionization trend in this area is likely to continue due to ongoing institutional overcrowding, safety, and parity concerns.

PROBATION AND PAROLE

With the unprecedented growth in the number of probation and parole clients, one would expect probation and parole officers to experience increased difficulty in performing their jobs. Caseloads have increased dramatically. More pre-sentence investigations are needed, more revocations are occurring, and more clients need increased supervision (Finn, 1984).

Johnson and Smith noted in 1981, that the number of unionized probation and parole agencies had grown from a total of three in 1972 to 19 (31.7%) in 1980. Because of increasing caseload trends, parity issues and other considerations, Johnson and Smith speculated that probation and parole personnel would continue to find unionization to be attractive during the 1980s.

It was also noted that the rapid expansion of unionization in probation and parole agencies could have interesting effects. Specifically, they speculated that unions would gain influence in areas such as hiring, probationary employment periods, promotion, and termination processes. Also, influence was anticipated in caseload ratios, training requirements for pre-service and in-service officers, overtime pay, special duty pay, other salary-related issues, and in matters of agency policy, objectives, and judicial decisions. These possibilities are even more cogent in view of the accelerated unionization trend.

With regard to the possibility of union influence on hiring, probation periods, promotion, and termination regulations in probation and parole agencies, the literature has shown that in some criminal justice agencies, contract negotiations with employee unions included these issues (Johnson and Smith, 1981).

The purpose of this research was to examine the current state of probation and parole unionization. Specifically, the authors updated material from Johnson and Smith's research on probation and parole unionization, and analyzed current data from a nationwide survey regarding the number of probation and parole agencies unionized; current probation and parole administrators' perceptions of the influence of unionization on cost of services, quality of services, and difficulty of administering services; and, current union influence on caseload, hiring and termination, training, fringe benefits, and administrative issues.

METHODOLOGY

In order to determine the current status of probation and parole unionization the authors conducted a survey of all state probation and parole agencies. Where such functions were locally administered, the appropriate policy agency was contacted.

Using the American Correctional Association Directory the names and addresses of all chief probation and parole administrators were identified, resulting in a population size of 65. The population size was more than 50 because of the division of probation and parole in many states into separate agencies. First, the number of unionized probation and parole agencies was determined. The "unionized" category included agencies where a union has sole collective bargaining rights, agencies where employees can join one of several unions with no sole collective bargaining right and, agencies where employees are represented by an employee organization that can collectively bargain for employees. Second, the survey ascertained probation and parole administrators' perceptions of the influence of unionization on cost of services, quality of services and difficulty of administering probation and parole services. Third, the survey assessed the influence of unionization on caseload, hiring and termination decisions, training requirements, fringe benefits, and administrative issues.

RESULTS

Sixty-three of the 65 agencies to which questionnaires were sent responded for a 97% response rate. The two agencies not responding were agencies which were locally administered. The authors were unable to identify an administrator capable or willing to respond to the questionnaire.

TABLE 1

Frequency of Union and Nonunion Agencies

	*1980		1988	
	n	%	n	%
**Union	19	31.7	36	57.1
***Nonunion	41	68.3	27	42.9

* 1980 is the baseline year since the data for the 1981 Johnson & Smith article were collected in 1980.

** "Union" includes union-with sole collective bargaining rights and multiple unions none with sole bargaining rights. 32 agencies were sole bargaining rights and 4 were multiple unions.

***Includes agencies with employee associations but without bargaining rights.

Of the 63 agencies responding, 36 (57.1%) were unionized. As Table 1 reflects, the 1980 survey indicated 19 agencies (31.7%) unionized. The only other research to examine probation and parole unionization was a 1972 study by Morton and Beadles which reported three probation and parole agencies unionized (Morton, et al., 1973).

TABLE 2

Agency Administrator Opinion of
Cost Impact of Unionization

	1980		1988	
	n	%	n	%
No Impact	19	31.7	6	9.5
Increase 1-5%	7	11.7	5	7.9
Increase 6-10%	13	21.7	10	15.9
Increase 11-15%	4	6.7	4	6.3
Increase Over 16%	7	11.7	1	1.6
No Response	10	16.7	37	58.7

As Table 2 reflects, administrators' opinions of the cost impact of unionization has changed markedly in two areas. The number of administrators responding "no impact" decreased from 19 (31.7% in 1980 to 6 (9.5%) in 1988. At the same time, "no response" increased from 10 (16.7%) in 1980 to 37 (58.7%) in 1988.

TABLE 3

Agency Administrator Opinion of
Quality Impact from Unionization

	1980		1988	
	n	%	n	%
No Impact	26	43.3	21	33.3
Positive Impact	11	18.3	10	15.9
Negative Impact	17	28.3	9	14.3
No Response	6	10.0	23	36.5

Administrators' perceptions of the impact of unionization on quality of services changed very little between 1980 and 1988. Table 3 reflects that the negative impact response decreased from 17 (28.3%) in 1980 to 9 (14.3%) in 1988. "No response", however, increased from 6 (10%) in 1980 to 23 (36.5%) in 1988.

TABLE 4

Agency Administrator Opinion of Administractive
Difficulty Impact from Unionization

	1980		1988	
	n	%	n	%
No Impact	24	40.0	13	20.6
Increase Difficulty	29	48.3	35	55.6

	1980		1988	
Decrease Difficulty	3	5.0	1	1.6
No Response	4	6.7	14	22.2

Regarding the impact of unionization on the difficulty of administering probation and parole services there was a decrease in the "no impact" response from 24 (40%) in 1980 to 13 (20.6%) in 1988. Also, "no response" increased from 4 (6.7%) in 1980 to 14 (22.2%) in 1988.

Perhaps the most striking results seen in Tables 2-4 are the high "no response" rates which did not appear in the results for less sensitive issues. Informal discussions with administrators in both union and non-union agencies indicated a general reluctance to make any statement which might be perceived as "combative" by union officials or pro-union employees. Agency administrators generally agreed (formally and informally) that unionization increased the difficulty of administrative jobs and made high administrative standards more difficult to achieve over the short term. Most, however, did not believe that unionization had a negative effect on the long term quality of performance of probation and parole agencies.

Regarding other issues, a majority of probation and parole administrators felt that union activity did not influence hiring and probationary evaluation policies for new officers, caseload size, overall agency goals, or judicial decision-making. A majority of administrators did indicate that union influence was significant in employee termination policies, promotion policies, and policies regarding in-service training for officers.

CONCLUSION

The increase in probation and parole unionization has occurred despite decreasing unionization in most other public sector areas. Membership has grown steadily from three agencies in 1972, as reported by Morton and Beadles, to nineteen agencies in 1981, to the current 36 agencies under union contract.

Informal discussions with probation and parole officers indicate a range of job related perceptions which may be relative to the appeal of unionization. Some officers describe a sense of hopelessness associated with large caseloads and the time required for investigative responsibilities. These officers feel that it is impossible to accomplish meaningful results under the current workload. Another frequent complaint concerns a perceived insensitivity on the part of administrators toward problems in controlling difficult clients. Often cited in this regard is administrative resistance to the revocation of violators whom the officers believe to be dangerous or in frequent disregard of the law. Finally, some officers have expressed a lack of confidence in administrator's support and a feeling that administrators are not likely to stand behind them when complaints, lawsuits, or salary questions arise.

If these perceptions are indeed widespread among probation and parole employees, then the unionization trend would be more easily explained.

Administrators explained the increased operating costs due to unionization as being primarily associated with increased man-hours devoted to personnel administration, and to a lesser degree, increases in employee pay and benefits. Indeed, salary levels and fringe benefits were not found to be significantly different between union and non-union agencies.

It appears, then, that the trend toward increased unionization in probation and parole is being driven by something beyond traditional salary and benefit concerns, and may indicate some deep structural flaws in the relationships between probation and parole employees, administrators, and state systems. In view of projections that probation and parole will play an increasingly important role in our correctional systems in the future, it is essential that these flaws be identified and remedied.

REFERENCES

Cole, George E., "The American System of Criminal Justice," 5th ed., Brooks/Cole Publishing Co., Monterey, California, 1989. See also, Smith, Barry D., Sapp, Allen D., "The Hidden Costs of Unionization and Collective Bargaining in Corrections," **Journal of Police and Criminal Psychology**, Vol. 1, No. 2, 1985.

Corrections Compendium, Contact Center Inc., December 1987. (Does not include California Probation which is estimated at approximately 2,000).

Finn, Peter, "Prison Crowding: The Response of Probation and Parole," **Crime and Delinquency**, 30, 1984.

Goldfield, Michael, "The Decline of Organized Labor in the United States," 1987. The University of Chicago Press.

Johnson, Charles L. and Smith, Barry. "Administrators' Perception of the Impact of Probation/Parole Employee Unionization, **Federal Probation**, March 1981.

Levin, David, Fenille, Peter and Kochan, Thomas. "Public Sector Labor Relations," 2nd ed., 1981, Thomas Horton and Daughters, Sun Lakes, Arizona. Also, Lipset, Seymour, "Unions in Transition," 1986, ICS Press, San Francisco, California.

Lipset, Seymour, "Unions in Transition," 1986. ICS Press, San Francisco, California.

Morton, Joann B., Callahan, Kirkwood, M., Beadles, Nicolas. Readings in Public Employment/Management Relations for Correctional Administration Corrections Division, Institute of Government, University of Georgia, Athens, 1973.

The National Manpower Survey of the Criminal Justice System, U.S. Department of Justice, LEAA, Washington, D.C., 1978.

Shafritz, Jay M. "Personnel Management in Government," 1986. Marcel Dekker, Inc., New York, New York.

Smith, Barry D., Sapp, Allen D., "The Hidden Costs of Unionization and Collective Bargaining in Corrections," **Journal of Police and Criminal Psychology**, Vol. 1, No. 2, 1985.

Sourcebook of Criminal Justice Statistics, U.S. Department of Justice, Bureau of Justice Statistics, Washington, D.C., 1987.

CHAPTER TEN

ETHICS OF CRIMINOLOGICAL RESEARCH
WITH CHILDREN AS SUBJECTS

Alexander B. Smith

Children are not small adults: they are highly impressionable individuals who need help in order to grow up properly. When researchers, in the name of advancing knowledge, choose children as experimental subjects, they should exercise all safeguards to avoid stigmatizing these children as delinquents.

In 1985 James Q. Wilson and Richard J. Herrnstein, then both of Harvard in **Crime and Human Behavior** *proposed identifying young children as predelinquents even though some of these children would be needlessly stigmatized. This was not the first time that prestigious college professors supported research aimed at labeling poor children as predelinquents even though these procedures were ineffective and resulted in children being erroneously labeled without the due process afforded by a juvenile court.*

INTRODUCTION

Children are not small adults; they are highly impressionable individuals who need help in order to grow up properly. When researchers, in the name of advancing knowledge, choose children as experimental subjects, they should exercise all safeguards to avoid stigmatizing these children as delinquents.

The history of criminology is a history of failed attempts by scientists, including social scientists, to develop a theory that will explain all, or a good portion of criminal behavior in single, simplistic terms. When attempts to prove untested theory remain in the classroom, no great harm is done. It is when proposals or suggestions are made to validate these theories by using human subjects, that because of obvious ethical considerations, great care must be taken. When the proposed subjects are children even greater care must be exercised.

Sometimes the attempts to develop theories have secured scholarly and media attention because of the novelty of their point of view. In 1928, Max G. Schlapp and Edwin H. Smith wrote, **The New Criminology** in which they advanced the thesis that crime was due to hormonal imbalance (Schlapp and Smith, 1928). While this concept initially attracted some attention, it was not supported by carefully conducted research. In 1965, Jacobs and her associates published a paper in which they reported that in a maximum security mental hospital in Scotland they found that a significant number of male prisoners who had "dangerous, violent or criminal tendencies, had abnormal sex chromosomes," XYY instead of XY (Jacobs, et al., 1965, pp. 1351-1352). However, many studies which attempted to validate this theory demonstrated that the XYY males were not predictably violent criminals (Witkin, et al., 1976, pp. 547-555). In both these cases, criminals were tested after conviction or adjudication to determine if there was a causal relationship between the behavior of the offender and the factor under investigation. I have made reference to these two theories only because they are representative of many studies which excited wide public interest when published, and held out what appeared to be easy solutions to the crime problem. In the above two instances no suggestions or proposals were made to screen large numbers of people to determine whether in the first case, they had hormonal problems, and in the second case, whether they had XYY chromosomes **before** they committed any crime. Wilson and Herrnstein cite studies of twins in order to prove that there is a genetic basis to criminal behavior. However, when these studies are subject to rigorous examination we find that genetic and environmental variables cannot be separated and interpretation becomes difficult (Bonn, 1984, pp. 108-110; Kamin, 1986, p. 24).

Every now and then students of crime "rediscover the wheel" and advance a theory or explanation of criminal behavior which had previously been laid to rest or which had only limited applicability. Then, depending on their PR abilities or their connections with prestigious universities they are given exposure by the media and frequently obtain large grants.

On August 4, 1985, the **New York Times Magazine** carried an article, "Are Criminals Made or Born?" by Harvard professors, Richard J. Herrnstein and James Q. Wilson (Professor Wilson is currently at UCLA) in which they summarized their "new" theory of crime causation as follows: "Evidence indicates that both biological and sociological factors play roles" (Herrnstein and Wilson, 1985, p. 31).

Had Professors Herrnstein and Wilson confined their **new** theory to professional conferences or classroom discussions I would have had no complaint. However, they have advanced a plan of identifying predelinquents using biological indicators when they are very young, because as they said, "chronic offenders typically begin their misconduct at an early age" (Herrnstein and Wilson, p. 46). They acknowledged that "...Prevention programs risk stigmatizing children, but this may be less of a risk than is neglect." They argued, "If stigma were a problem to be avoided at all costs, we would have to dismantle most special-needs educating programs." (It is difficult for me to accept this parallel. Stigmatizing a child as a predelinquent or delinquent is far more traumatic than identifying a child as having a problem in learning how to read or to do arithmetic.)

From reading the Herrnstein and Wilson **New York Times** article and their book **Crime and Human Nature** (Wilson and Herrnstein, 1985), it is clear that they have carefully researched the relevant literature. They cited many important books and articles, including publications and studies by the Harvard Law School's seminal criminological researchers and scholars, Sheldon and Eleanor Glueck. However, they apparently were not aware that prior to 1950, the Gluecks developed the "Glueck Prediction Scale" which listed a number of elements in rating children in order to identify predelinquents. Using the Glueck scale, the New York City Youth Board and the Maximum Benefits Project of Washington, D.C. each designed programs aimed at identifying predelinquent children in certain schools in their respective cities, and then followed the careers of these previously identified children to determine the validity of the scale. (Note: The scale devised by the Gluecks had been derived from retrospective analyses of known institutionalized delinquents and nondelinquents and was aimed at rating the familial relationships and environments of the children.)

In 1965, M. M. Craig and S. J. Glick of the New York City Youth Board enthusiastically reported the results of utilizing the Glueck Scale in the selected New York City Schools, saying, "It has yielded a sufficient degree of accuracy to warrant its use by those agencies interested in delinquency prevention and control" (Craig and Glick, 1965, p. 175). However, the critics who analyzed and studied the data were dismayed by the inaccuracy of the report and the dangers of its implications in incorrectly labeling many children as predelinquent. The main criticism was articulated by Professor Alfred J. Kahn (Kahn, 1965) of the Columbia School of Social Work who called attention to the immorality of labeling a child as a predelinquent without the due process afforded by a juvenile court. He also demonstrated that the Glueck scale was inaccurate and ineffective in identifying the target children.

I fully understand that Herrnstein and Wilson were concerned with biological factors and not the Glueck Prediction Scale which included social factors in identifying predelinquents. However, the degree of care required for safeguarding little children who are the focus of research from being labeled delinquent is the same no matter what techniques are employed. Other people's children require the same degree of freedom from needless risk as one's own. When these two professors acknowledge "that there is at present little hard evidence that we know how to inhibit the development of delinquent tendencies in children," I believe that they should have been more careful in proposing research which had not been pretested and which deals with subjects who are so defenseless. Academics who have access to prestigious media have a duty of weighing their pronouncements carefully because harm might result when certainly none was intended.

A critical concern in using children as subjects in any kind of experimentation is that they are unable to give "informed consent" which conforms to a model, the elements of which are: information, competence, understanding, voluntariness, and decision (Litz, et al., p. 5). Even when we propose research with adult criminals we must be sensitive to the possibility that they might be harmed merely by being subjects in an experiment. The law is clear that when an adult criminal willingly requests experimental surgery, the request will not be approved **pro forma**. In **Kaimowitz v. Department of Mental Health** (1973) the court blocked a plan initiated by a prison inmate to have psychosurgery performed so that he might no longer be a danger to society and consequently might not have to serve the remainder of a life sentence as an adjudicated sexual psychopath. The reason given by the court was that in the inherently coercive atmosphere of confinement the petitioner could not give **informed consent** (emphasis mine).

There is universal agreement that from a legal as well as from an ethical standpoint, the decision in **Kaimowitz** was constitutional and proper. I do not suggest that the development of theory should be needlessly inhibited or curtailed. However, I urge that researchers be vigilant and extra careful, particularly when dealing with children. In many cases children are not in a position to give consent, informed or otherwise. Our culture which is reflected in our laws, demands that children be handled with a greater degree of care than adults. Our scientists and social scientists should anticipate the possible harm to which they may subject children by the process of labeling them delinquents.

The children who were tested in New York City using the Glueck Scale were drawn from the economically deprived, high crime areas of East Harlem. As it is, because of a host of economic, social, health and other problems and disadvantages, it is remarkable that so many children in this and similar areas grow up without a criminal record. We should, if at all possible, refrain from labeling these children as predelinquent. The predelinquent label, needlessly applied is an additional handicap that a developing child does not need.

I want to call your attention to a portion of the history of the juvenile courts from their inception in 1899 to the middle 1960's. During that time we saw how these courts, set up in behalf and for the benefit of children, deviated from their laudable purpose and, in many parts of the United States, deteriorated so that they became no more than "kangaroo courts" (a description used by Justice Fortas in **In re Gault**, 1967). In **Kent v. United States** (1966, at 555-556), the first case heard by the U.S. Supreme Court which dealt with the absence cf procedural rights of children in juvenile courts, Justice Fortas commented:

> There is evidence, in fact, that there may be grounds for concern that the child receives the worst of both worlds; that he gets neither the protection accorded to adults nor the solicitous care and regenerative treatment postulated for children.

We need to exercise special care so that we never arrive at a position where we have needlessly harmed children. Our record of benign neglect with respect to the juvenile courts from 1899 to 1966 should not be paralleled by our subsequent lack of sensitivity to the ethics of experimenting with children. Nor should it become necessary for the courts to extricate social scientists from problems that may arise when our highest ethical considerations do not control our research with children as subjects.

REFERENCES

Bonn, Robert. **Criminology.** New York: McGraw-Hill, 1984.

Craig, Maude M. and S. J. Glick, "Application of the Glueck Social Prediction Table on an Ethnic Basis," **Crime and Delinquency,** April 1965.

In re Gault, 387 U.S. 1 (1967).

Herrnstein, Richard J. and James Q. Wilson, "Are Criminals Made or Born?" **New York Times Magazine,** August 4, 1985.

Jacobs, Patricia A., Muriel Brunton, and Maria Melville, "Aggressive Behavior, Mental Subnormality, and the XYY Male, **Nature,** 208, December 1965.

Kahn Albert J., "The Case of Premature Claims: Public Policy and Delinquency Prediction," **Crime and Delinquency,** 11, 3, July 1965.

Kaimowitz v. Dept. of Mental Health, Civ. Action No. 73-19434 - AW (Cir. Ct. Wayne County, Mich. filed July 10, 1973).

Kamin, Leon, J., "Is Crime in the Genes? The Answer May Depend on Who Chooses What Evidence," **Scientific American,** Feb. 1986.

Kent v. United States, 383 U.S. 541 (1966).

Litz, Charles W., Alan Meisel, Eviatar Zerubavel, Mary Carter, Regina M. Sestak, and Loren H. Roth. **Informed Consent: A Study of Decision making in Psychiatry.** N.Y.: Guilford PRess, 1984.

Schlapp, Max A. and Edward H. Smith. **The New Criminology.** New York: Liveright, 1928.

Wilson, James Q. and Richard J. Herrnstein. **Crime and Human Nature.** New York: Simon and Schuster, 1985.

Witkin, et al., "Criminality in XYY and XXY Men," **Science,** 193, August 13, 1976, pp. 547-555.

CHAPTER ELEVEN

SOME OBSERVATIONS OF THE STATUS AND PERFORMANCE OF FEMALE CORRECTIONS OFFICERS IN MEN'S PRISONS

Judith D. Simon

and

Rita J. Simon

The observations of a young female officer about the role of female guards in men's prisons and the interaction between male and female guards in those prisons are the major foci of this article. The conclusions reached are that women officers carry their weight in men's prisons and that most of the inmates like having female officers around. They humanize the institution.

INTRODUCTION

This article focuses on two controversial issues concerning female roles in the criminal justice system: the quality of the interaction between male and female corrections officers: and the relationships between inmates and female officers. It examines such issues as the reported resentment on the part of male officers at having to work with women. There is the feelings on their part that women officers could not hold their own in difficult or tense situations. There exist the additional feeling in the prison, men would not only have to protect themselves, and get the situation under control, but would have the additional worry of looking after their women colleagues. Male guards have been quoted as saying, "Rather than having the protection of a buddy working along side me, we have an extra burden--that of looking after the women officers."[1]

The data for this article stems primarily from the observations of a young, middle class, white woman who worked in a men's medium security prison for 13 months as a corrections officer. Altogether there were 150 corrections officers in this prison, about 40 of whom were women; only two of whom were white. The administrative staff consisted of the warden, two assistant deputy wardens, the inspector, three captains, six lieutenants, and 10 sergeants. With the exception of two female lieutenants and one sergeant, the rest were males. The first woman corrections officer had been hired about a decade earlier in the late 1970s. Prior to that, women had worked in the prison as teachers, secretaries, nurses, and in social service capacities.

Built originally as a city house of corrections, the state took over the facility in 1985. The state retained all the city employees but required they undergo an extensive training program the same as any new state corrections officer (or non-custody workers) would undergo. Of the city employees, more than half left the facility and took other positions in civil service.

Of those who chose to remain and work for the state, half quit within several months after the state took over. The few that did not quit report that those who left did not like the more restrictive rules and regulations imposed by the state. They felt that they were stripped of much of their power and authority over prisoners, leaving them in a dangerous situation. For example, under the city rules, the guards were permitted to carry weapons with them inside the facility, but under the state rules, no weapons were permitted inside the perimeters other than during riot conditions. The city guards were also upset at the loss of many services that the prisoners used to provide them free of charge such as haircuts, shoe shines, and car washes. When the facility was run by the city there were no women guards. There was one woman sergeant, a former city police officer, and there were a number of women who worked in a social service capacity.

The inmate population in the fall of 1986 was 650; a year later the number had been reduced to 500, the maximum permitted under state regulations. Under the state classification system, the facility is a medium security prison which specializes in parole violators. That means that most of the inmates have served time earlier and were somewhat older than the typical state prisoner. The offenses for which they violated their parole are primarily drug related property crimes. There was also a fairly large group of violent offenders who had been found guilty of murder, manslaughter, armed robbery, and aggravated assault. At least 80 percent of the inmates were black, there was a small group of Hispanics, and all the others were white males.

The Tasks Assigned Male and Female Guards

There was no difference between the duties and responsibilities of the male and female commanding officers. They included scheduling the custody staff, reviewing and updating employee personnel files, insuring that the daily operations of the prison ran smoothly, and filing reports on all critical incidents. Additionally, the commanders reviewed disciplinary "tickets" (reports) that officers wrote on the prisoners, occasionally heard prisoners' complaints, and monitored the on-the-job training of new officers. One member of the command staff was required to monitor each meal in the dining hall, and at least once during their eight hour shift, they made rounds, and inspected all the housing units. There was one commander in the control center at all times.

According to Department of Corrections policy, commanding officers were supposed to assign staff to positions without consideration of the officer's sex. The extent to which this policy was followed depended on which commander was doing the scheduling. At the beginning of one of the author's employ in the prison, she observed that women were assigned either to the information desk, the control center or the front gate; men were always assigned to the arsenal, the alert response vehicles, and the yard. After a few months, a change was men as well as women were regularly assigned to the information desk and the control center. Women were just as likely to be assigned to the arsenal and to the alert response vehicles as were the male officers. The changes seemed to be the result of an influx of new officers and other changes in the command staff that are described below.

There was a dramatic difference between the attitudes of the men who had recently completed the training academy and those who had either been with the state for many years or had worked for the city. The men who were newer to the system generally accepted women as equals and respected the women officers and commanders. There was a sense of camaraderie and teamwork between the young officers (in experience, not necessarily in years) who completed the academy. But since the academy had only been in existence for a few years there were only a limited number of officers who shared that experience. These men exhibited almost no animosity toward their female colleagues nor did they complain that they were incompetent. That is to not to say that they did not complain about a particular woman, but the complaints did not stem from the officer being a woman. The male guards who had either worked for the city or had been with the state for many years were more likely to resent women generally and many of these officers indicated that they would have preferred that women not work inside the prison at all.

Many of the women were housing unit officers. They were in charge of running a unit of 40-55 men for eight hours. The yard crew, frequently all male officers, were in charge of relieving these unit officers for their restroom breaks as well as their regular meal breaks. Often times the yard crew would complain that the women officers would demand many more restroom reliefs than the male officers. These men would accuse the women of demanding these breaks even when they did not need to use the restroom. It is possible that the women did abuse the system however, it is important to note that the male officers often did not ask for restroom reliefs because they were able to use the restrooms in the housing units since the prisoners and the guards were all men. The only women's restrooms were located in the kitchen and in the administration building.

Situations occurred several times a week when an officer would call the control center asking for assistance or complaining that he/she was having difficulty managing the unit. Other times a member of the yard crew who arrived at a housing unit to relieve a regular officer would notify the control center that the unit was out of control. These problems occurred more frequently with male officers than with female officers. There were several men and women who had problems controlling their units on a regular basis and there seemed to be no solution for these officers other than to assign them to posts with less inmate contact. Additionally, there were some officers who could not carry out their duties properly whatever their assignment. Here too the problems occurred more often with men than with women officers. The commanders were well aware of these problems and of the problem officers. But the commanders rarely made generalized statements indicating one gender of officers was preferable over another. The shift commander occasionally remarked that women officers had a better overall record of reporting for work on time than men officers did. One explanation offered was that the woman officers were less likely "to stay out drinking until late at night." The occasions when women officers failed to report to work were usually because their children were sick or other family problems presented themselves.

Occasionally, there were disturbances in the yard or in the housing units that required several officers to respond immediately. All officers who were in a position to do so were expected to respond: men and women alike. As a general rule, officers were anxious to come to the aid of their fellow officers and responded quickly. However, there were some officers who were notorious for disappearing during emergencies. There were several men and women who enjoyed this reputation. There were also men and women officers whom their fellow officers preferred not to have on the scene. Generally the male officers who were not welcomed were feared because they tended to get the prisoners riled up and to escalate the situation. The unwelcomed women officers were not desired because they were ineffective. The prisoners made fun of these women; and thus, it was more difficult to quell the disturbance.

The Reactions of the Inmates to Female Guards

In general, the prisoners tended to relate to each officer as an individual. They tried to play on the officer's weaknesses in the hops of receiving favorable treatment, or of getting the officer to do favors for them, or of allowing them to get away with prohibited acts. The prisoners played on women officers' appearance or sex appeal by complimenting them, by making suggestive remarks, and by asking a lot of personal questions. They would try to make all new officers, and in particular the woman officer feel uncomfortable and frightened, hoping that these feelings would prompt the officer to seek out friendships with the prisoners. The prisoners would then use these friendships to their benefit, starting out perhaps with extra portions at meals, or extra phone time and leading to sexual favors, or even complicity in escape. For the first several weeks the prisoners seem to pull out all the stops to try and "set up" a new officer, be it a man or a woman. They tried hard to treat the officer as a "special" person.

But a prisoner's primary concern is his personal safety and the safety of his belongings. Any other preferences or desires are secondary to these concerns for survival and safety. Thus, any consideration a prisoner might give to liking a male or female officer is secondary to his concern that the officer be able and willing to protect him and his property.

Protecting the prisoners does not necessarily involve great physical strength or size; rather it involves the guard's ability to maintain order and enforce the prison's rules. Initially, prisoners are skeptical of any officer's ability to maintain order. Once an officer proves him or herself, most prisoners are ready to accept that officer. Some prisoners do not like women in general; and they may especially resent women in positions of authority. Some think all women officers are reformed prostitutes (once the state did hire many ex-prostitutes). Still others dislike women officers because they claim that some women purposely set out to tease them and thus are a source of great frustration e.g., women who wear their clothes too tight, use too much make-up, have on too much jewelry. Finally, there are those who dislike certain women officers because they think they are too "manly", indicating they are lesbians. These inmates are unwilling to concede that a woman officer is able to maintain order and they cause trouble whenever a woman is in charge. But they are a small minority of the inmates.

Once a woman officer establishes her competency, many of the prisoners are pleased to have her in place of a man. Many of the inmates believe that women treat them with more respect and more care than the male guards. They believe that the women guards do not need to constantly affirm their power over the prisoners, as opposed to the male officers who see power and control as symbols of their manhood. Many of the prisoners are also more anxious to talk to women officers about their personal situation; once they are past their initial "wooing" stage.

The Authority Wielded by Prison Gurards

In his account of social interactions and patterns of authority in total institutions Erving Goffman observed that any staff member, no matter how lowly his or her status, can exercise power over any inmate/patient in the institution irrespective of the inmate's or patient's prior role in the larger society (Goffman, 1961). As observed in the prison, this authority is particularly evident in one-on-one confrontations between a prisoner and an officer. An officer may lose a particular battle. He may not, for example, succeed in forcing a prisoner to turn over a piece of contraband at a particular moment but he always wins the war, because in the end it is the officer's word against the inmate's word. He will get the contraband from the prisoner.

Each officer usually comes up with his/her own standards, about how much discretion to exercise. Some believe that the best way to do their job, is to be nice to the prisoners, to do little extras. After all, if you are nice to them, they will be nice to you. In the training academy, instructors try to discourage this approach because they believe it is dangerous.

Some prisoners become angry that others are getting special treatment, just by asking. Those who become angry will not ask; it is against their prison code. Prisoners are frightened and feel insecure if the rules are not enforced strictly. Their fear also makes them angry. Other officers try to cultivate a few friendships, hoping that these prisoners will come to their aid if there is trouble. This, too, is discouraged by the training staff because it is rare for a prisoner to openly protect an officer at the expense of another prisoner since this is likely to lead to retaliation by "friends" of the injured prisoner.

Still other officers adopt the style of enforcing the rules to the fullest extent such as writing a ticket when a violation occurs, not negotiating with the prisoner once a violation has taken place, and treating all prisoners the same. It is often the case that these officers write the fewest tickets; after their brief initial period when they have established control by writing lots of tickets and have gained the prisoners' respect for their authority. The prisoners are more likely to respond to these officers' requests and demands and they are more likely to adhere to prison rules when these officers are in charge.

Concluding Remarks

In sum, our overall assessment about whether women correction's officers carry their weight in a men's prison and whether they are accepted by their male colleagues and the male inmates is positive. A male officer's position is neither threatened nor endangered by having to work along side a female officer. Female officers are as likely to assume their responsibilities, stand up to the prisoners, and enforce the rules as male officers are; and for the most part the male and female officers recognize the absence of differences. As for the prisoners, most of them like having women around; it humanizes the institution.

ENDNOTE

1. For further discussion of these issues see: Lynn Zimmer, 1986, WOMEN GUARDING MEN, Chicago: University of Chicago Press; Clarice Feinman, 1980, WOMEN IN THE CRIMINAL JUSTICE SYSTEM, New York: Praeger; Nicole Hahn Rafter and Elizabeth A. Stanko, 1982, WOMEN, GENDER ROLES AND CRIMINAL JUSTICE, Boston: Northeastern University Press.

REFERENCE

Goffman, Erving. 1961. **Asylum: Essays on the Social Situations of Mental Patients and Other Inmates.** Garden City, New York: Anchor Books.

CHAPTER TWELVE

A STUDY OF PATROL DEPLOYMENT ALLOCATION FOR THE SAVANNAH POLICE DEPARTMENT

Michael J. Palmiotto

and

George G. Padgett

Patrol has been called the backbone of a police department. They are the initial recipients of all citizens' complaints and the first to arrive at the scene of a crime. The patrol tasks cover as wide range of activities that can be considered highly complex. The patrol unit has the responsibility of responding in an appropriate manner to numerous incidents assigned to them by their communications section.

The National Advisory Commission on Criminal Justice Standards and Goals, Task Force on Police in 1973 recommended that "every police agency immediately should develop a patrol deployment system that is responsive to the demands for police services and consistent with the effective use of the agency's patrol personnel."

This article evaluates patrol deployment plans from pre-1983 through the 1988 patrol deployment plan. Experience at Savannah Police has shown that the best beat structures were those that used the most recent dispatch data as a prediction of when, where, and how many officers would be needed next year. The method and formula used was less important than complete accurate data applied with a knowledge of the geography of the city as well as the use of common sense.

Patrol has been called the backbone of a police department. They are the initial recipients of all citizen complaints and the first to arrive at the scene of a crime. The patrol tasks cover a wide range of activities that can be considered highly complex. The patrol unit has the responsibility of responding in an appropriate manner to numerous incidents assigned to them by their communications section.

In developing a patrol deployment data base, the first phase requires determining the activities of the patrol force. They can be divided into four categories: call for service, preventive patrol, officer--initiated activities, and administrative tasks (Gay, 1977, p. 3).   In reviewing Police Patrol workload studies, Gary Cordner (1979, p. 58) concluded that:

1. A large portion of calls to the police are handled without dispatching a patrol unit (30-70%).

2. Of the calls radioed to patrol units:
   a. only a small portion are, narrowly defined, crime-related;

   b. only a small portion are, narrowly defined, law-enforcement-related;

   c. only a small portion are, narrowly defined, non-crime-related;

   d. a large portion are ambiguous in nature.

3. About one-half of patrol time is uncommitted, during which patrol officers have wide latitude in determining what to do.

4. Patrol officers spend a substantial portion of their total time (10-20%) on non-duty activities, such as taking breaks.

5. Patrol officers spend a substantial but widely varying portion of their total time (10-50%) on administrative activities. To what extent this variation is an artifact of different definitions is not clear.

The National Advisory Commission on Criminal Justice Standards and Goals, Task Force on Police recommended in 1973 that "every police agency immediately should develop a patrol deployment system that is responsive to the demands for police services and consistent with the effective use of the agency's patrol personnel" (Task Force on Police, 1973, p. 199). In addition, the Task Force also recommended that police departments collect and analyze data and perform work load studies before deploying patrol personnel. The patrol force usually requires the greatest resources of a municipal police department and most of a department's police personnel, usually 70 percent or more of its sworn manpower. Because of these factors the goal of police agencies should be the efficient deployment of its patrol services. Police departments should be concerned with planning and managing of their patrol force. Patrol deployment requires sound management which enables administrators to keep abreast of how patrol resources are used. This allows the managers to identify problems and to determine appropriate changes. By establishing patrol allocation, planning police administrators are provided an opportunity to monitoring patrol activities such as calls for service. **Patrol Deployment,** a study sponsored by the National Institute of Justice, advocates that when planning patrol allocation the following questions confront a police department:

How many patrol units should be on duty during each shift?

How should they be distributed among the various communities in the city or county?

Should one officer or two be assigned to each car? Or, should there be a mix of one-officer and two-officer cars?

How do patrol officers spend their time when they are not handling calls for service?

What are the patrol beats for each car?

Which citizen calls merit response by a patrol car, and which ones can be handled by other means, such as taking a crime report over the telephone?

How many cars are dispatched to each call?

What should be the starting times of patrol officers' tours of duty?

What do patrol officers' schedules look like: days on duty, tour rotations, and so forth (Levine and McEwen, 1985, p. 3).

In evaluating patrol plans, the preceding questions can aid in collecting and analyzing data and measuring patrol performance. By routinely planning patrol allocation the benefits derived are: greater control of patrol resources, more efficient delivery of police services, and enhanced information for decision making (Levine et al., p. 3).

This article studies the patrol allocation for the Savannah, Georgia Police Department as a case in point. Since 1983 the Savannah Police Department has utilized five different patrol beat structures. Each beat structure was arrived at by using a different method. Also, each method is reviewed and evaluated as to how it met the call for service or crime patterns. This study also discusses the difficulty of structuring beats, amount of time to structure each beat, response time, and factors to be considered when developing a beat structure.

CASE STUDY:

City of Savannah

The city is located on the south eastern coast line of Georgia. The city has an hourglass shape due to the location of Hunter

Army Airfield on the west and the sea marsh on the east. The Savannah River is the northern boundary of the city and serves as the access to a major sea port. The city is 12 miles by 8 miles of flat land which has been divided into compartments by railroad tracks and drainage canals.

The population of Savannah is approximately 147,000 with a 53.2 percent non-white population. The school enrollment makes up 26.1% of the total population. The Historic area of the city has an official population of 7,021. However, the day time population has been estimated at 20,000 and even higher during special holiday events such as Saint Patrick's Day where the population in the Historic area may exceed 100,000. The Victorian area of Savannah, a tourist attraction due to its Victorian style housing, has experienced wide changes in daily and hourly population counts.

Savannah Police Department

The police department has been divided into four divisions, each commanded by a major. These are: Field Operations, Criminal investigations, Staff Services, and Auxiliary and Technical Services. Field Operations is further subdivided into four sections, each under the command of a Captain. Three Captains oversee three watches with one Captain responsible for the Special operations unit. The Special Operations Unit contains the Traffic Unit, Tactical Response and Prevention Unit, forty-eight civilian school crossing guards, special walking beats, the Crime Prevention Unit, the Warrant Team, the Vice-Squad, the Historic Area Horse Patrol, and several Mini-Stations located in the public housing projects.

Field Operations contain 243 officers and 52 civilians of the 328 Officers and 136 civilians authorized for the department. There are 156 non-supervisory level sworn officers to patrol the city. These officers are divided among three shifts to fill the 78 patrol beats and 7 wagons that are staffed during a 24 hour period. There is a total of 22 sergeants and four lieutenants under the control of the three Watch Captains. These ranking officers are responsible for supervising the field patrol officers.

Pre-1983 Patrol Beat Plan

The plan used prior to December of 1983 was based upon the number of calls in each area of the city. There were three watches as follows:

1st Shift - 23 beats, midnight to 7:59 A.M., 42 beat officers.

2nd Shift - 23 beats, 8:00 A.M. to 3:59 P.M., 42 beat officers.

3rd Shift - 35 beats, 4:00 P.M. to 11:59: P.M., 62 beat officers.

A study conducted in early 1983 found that the manpower allocation for each shift matched the workload to within 4 percent. The details describing the exact method used to plan the best pattern for each shift is no longer available. The maps that depict the beat boundaries for each shift are available, and it is apparent that call-for-service data was used. The beats are concentrated in the areas of the city where crime was the most concentrated. The planners followed man-made and natural obstacles as beat boundaries. The shift change times were chosen to match manpower to workload. By the end of 1983, the beat pattern was no longer operating as planned and was reevaluated.

December 1983 Patrol Beat Plan

The plan used from 1984 through 1985 was the result of a study conducted by the International Association of Chiefs of Police in December 1983. The method used a 10 percent systematic sample of all calls over the twelve month period of 1 August 1982 to 31 July 1983. The city was divided into 188 reporting areas. The data collected included the time of day, day of week, type of incident, the reporting area, and the number of arrests. The shift change times were based upon the work per hour chart. A weighted average formula was used to "score" each reporting area. These scores were then plotted on three maps, each representing the activity of one shift. The reporting areas were then grouped into beats of equal workload.

The IACP study made two assumptions. First, they assumed that the average call required 45 minutes of the officer's time. Second, they believed that a beat officer should only expend one third of his or her eight hour shift on calls for service. The other two-thirds would be for preventative patrol, administrative duties, and a buffer for when the calls were received at a more than normal rate. This was to prevent calls from being "stacked" and dispatched later.

Since each beat would require 2,920 man-hours (365 x 8) of patrol each year, the study recommended a beat distribution of:

First Shift	32 beats
Second Shift	33 beats
Third Shift	52 beats
TOTAL	117 beats

Additionally, a study of the availability of officers resulted in a ratio of 1.66 officers assigned to patrol for one officer on duty each shift. This factor, when applied to the 117 recommended beats, indicated that 194 beat officers were needed. This was 48 more than the number currently being used to do the job. This would have been a 33 percent increase in the size of the patrol force. It was not financially feasible to increase the size of the department at that time. Additionally, the fact that the calls for service were being answered by the current level of manpower proved that the assumptions were not entirely valid. The manpower for beats has been increased to 156 over a four year period. The size of the Special Operations Unit has also grown.

The patrol beat plan finally used was based upon the current strength and the weighted scores of each reporting area.

1985 Patrol Deployment Plan

The beat pattern was designed utilizing a weighted average of all primary and back up dispatches. The average total time expended by both the primary and backup officers for certain types of calls was used as the weighting factor in the calculation. The weighted average method was used because complete detailed data was not available. The city was divided into 288 reporting areas. The score of each reporting area was computed as follows:

Score (RP) = [(% Populations) (Weighting FactorPop.)+

(% Accidents-W/Injuries) (W.F.Acc.-W/Inj.)+

(% Accidents-W/Injuries) (W.F.Acc.-W/O Inj.)+

(% Homicides) (W.F. Hom.)+

(% Rape) (W.F. Rap.)+

(% Robbery((W.F.Rob.)+

(% Aggrevated Assault) (W.F.A.A.)+

(% Burglary) (W.F.Bur.)+

(% Larceny((W.F.Lar.)+

(% Calls for Service) (Combined Average
Time Spent Per Call) (W.F.Time)+

(% Arrests) (W.F.Arr.)] / TOTAL of all
W.F.'s

Weighting factors were assigned based on importance, average time consumption per incident, and difficulty of servicing the call. The shift score was then computed as a total of all reporting area scores for that shift. The number of patrol officers that should be assigned to a shift was computed as follows:

Officers per shift =   Shift Score   X Total Patrol

                       Grand Total Score   Officers

The number arrived at was the number of officers per shift that could be assigned without hiring more officers for patrol.

Designing Beat Boundaries: The reporting area scores were plotted on an overlay for each shift. The total number of patrol officers for each shift was divided by the department's assignment/availability factor. The resulting quotient, rounded to the nearest whole number, was the number of beats that can be maintained with the officers assigned to the shift. The total shift score was then divided by the number of beats. The answer was a beat score.

The final step in beat design was to draw boundaries that encompass reporting areas with a total score close to the beat score and which takes into consideration the natural and man-made boundaries marked on the overlay. Zones were then drawn by combining beats under the control of a sergeant. This method required one analyst to work three months at twenty hours a week to complete.

The 1986 Patrol Deployment Plan

Beginning in January, 1986, a twenty beat plan was placed into operation. This plan was developed without the use of dispatch data. This plan required the work of one person for 8 hours to complete. The plan had several major guidelines.

1. There would be three shifts.

2. The shifts would change at midnight, 8:00 A.M., and 4:00 P.M.

3. The number of officers on each shift would be: 45, 45, and 66.

4. There would be twenty beats on each shift and the same pattern would be used for all shifts.

5. The captain of each shift would decide daily where to deploy the officers in excess of the twenty basic beat officers.

6. The city would be divided into three zones; each zone containing several beats under one sergeant.

7. The beat size was determined by dividing the city into twenty nearly equal size beats using major roads and canals as the boundaries.

8. The morning and day shifts would rotate personnel at the beginning of each month, the evening shift would not exchange personnel.

The plan provided each captain with a basic twenty beat plan. The captain had to deploy as many as sixteen additional officers each day based upon the shift captain's own evaluation of the most recent crime pattern.

1987 Patrol Deployment Plan

The plan was implemented in January of 1988. This plan utilized only the time expended by primary officers in each reporting area. Theory being that the more time expended on a call, the more serious the call was. This automatically weighted the calls and no formula was needed.

The beat structure of a police department is necessary for command and control of the patrol units. The beat plan should distribute units throughout the city so that each unit will have the minimum travel time to incident locations and so that preventative patrol can be provided where needed.

The beat structure was designed after a comprehensive study of all police activities in a three month period had been made. First, the amount of work required in man-minutes was determined for each hour of the day for each day of the week. Had the weekend activity differed greatly from the weekday activity, two separate plans would have been needed. Second, using the amount of work required for each hour of the day, the number of units required per hour was determined. This information was then graphed. From the pattern of activity, the shift change times and the number of units required for each shift were determined. Once the shift change times were established and the number of units required for each shift had been determined, the beat pattern for each shift was determined. The city map was divided into 1175 "XY" squares that are approximately 1000 feet on each side. All of the data entered into the mainframe was coded with the XY for the location of occurrence. By focusing only on the time period of one shift, the total length of time actually expended in each XY was computed. These totals were then plotted by XY on a large map of the city. The grand total of time expended for the shift was divided by the total number of units required thus arriving at the average total time expended by each unit. This average was then used to group the XY totals into beats of equal total time. The boundaries of each beat take into account the natural and man-made terrain features such as canals, railroad tracks, interstate highways, and major arteries of traffic flow.

The Computer Aided Dispatch system caused the Savannah Police Department plan to be even more complicated. The CAD system does not use XY's; instead it uses the Metropolitan Planning Unit's reporting areas. The Reporting Areas (RA's) are of uneven size and are not numbered in a manner that makes plotting easy. The RA's do have one advantage over the XY system. The RA's follow the roads, canals, and major arteries for boundaries whereas the XY's use only straight line running vertical and horizontal on a map. In order to design the Savannah Police Department beat system, the beats were first designed utilizing the XY grid system and then converted into a pattern that was a "best fit" to the RA system the CAD system requires to operate on. Because of the oddly shaped RA's, some of the resulting beat boundaries were not logical when viewed from the street officer's perspective. It was imperative that the shifts use the maps given to them for the shift period they were designed for. The patterns for the Day and Night shifts appeared to be close enough to be interchangeable. **THEY WERE NOT!** The CAD system dispatched calls in a manner that resulted in each unit having approximately the same amount of work. This also insured that each unit had approximately the same amount of time available for preventative patrol. Individual units could have ruined this strategic plan by patrolling the wrong area even though the CAD system dispatched the unit to the correct area. Units doing this could have left some areas of the city not patrolled and other areas having more preventative patrol time than required because of units overlapping.

The current beat structure was evaluated in April 1988 after the CAD system had recorded three months of data on the 1987 beat structure. Using the same method described above, the beat workload was determined. Since the workload was no longer of near equal distribution, the beat structure for that shift was redesigned.

1988 Patrol Deployment Plan

The beat structure was designed to equalize the workload among officers and to place officers in the areas that statistically have proven to be the most active for the period of day that the officer is working. It also had to satisfy the requirements imposed by city officials and police managers. These constraints are developed as a result of Charts 1-3. The call for service data used was the most comprehensive of all the previous patrol deployment plans. The data used was 100% of the primary and backup dispatchers for 84 days of continuous operations. The actual time expended on each case was used for the calculation. A weighted average was not used. The man-minutes plotted on the city map were the actual total time expended in that area of the city during the 84 day period. There was no unusual activities during this period such as Christmas holiday or Saint Patrick's Day celebrations that would distort the data. Because the Computer Aided Dispatch system records all activity (calls for service, officer initiated calls, preventative patrol, and administrative duties); it was possible for the first time to compute the percentage of time that each beat would devote to answering calls, and how much time would be available for preventative patrol.

CHART I

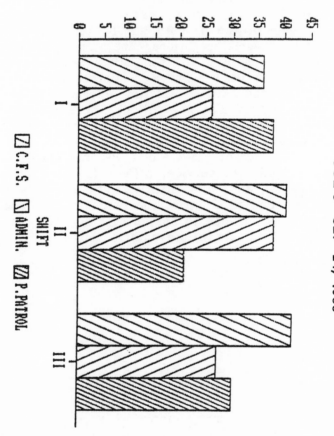

This was used to further modify the beat structure to increase the preventative patrol time in the areas that had a high burglary and robbery count. Workload and manpower were not balanced in order that more preventative patrol time could be concentrated on first and third shifts.

CHART 2

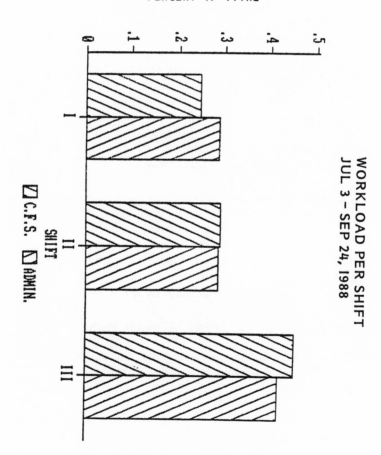

This plan required approximately 100 man-hours to complete. Of the 100, 24 hours were personal computer design time.

Guidelines for December 1988 Patrol Deployment Plan

The new beat pattern was developed to service the community when and where police services were needed as revealed by studying all dispatch records of the preceding three months. The beat plan was adjusted to meet the need for additional preventative patrol time on some shifts and in some areas of the city. To accomplish this, consideration was given as to when and where the serious crimes occurred. After analysis of the call-for-service data, the following guidelines were set by the City Manager, Chief of Police, and Patrol Operations Commander:

1. The city would be patrolled by three non-overlapping shifts.

2. The shifts would be for an eight hour duration.

3. The shift changes would be at midnight, 8:00 A.M. and 4:00 P.M.

4. The number of officers on the First and Second shifts would be the same so that the two shifts could rotate every month.

5. The number of beats on First shift and Second shift would be the same so that the two shifts could rotate at the beginning of each month.

6. The city would be divided into four zones.

7. Each zone would be assigned to a sergeant with officers assigned to beats inside of each zone.

8. The zone boundaries would be the same for each of the three shifts.

9. The zone boundaries for Zone II would follow those of the Historic and Victorian areas.

10. Zone II would receive special coverage due to the high concentration of serious crimes in that area.

11. The number of wagons for each shift would be two, two, and three respectively.

12. The data from traffic accident would only be used if the accident was answered by a patrol unit and not a special traffic unit.

13. The only data used would be that recorded for patrol units. The data for sergeants, wagons, and special units would not be included.

14. The total time that the officer was involved in the case would be utilized. This would represent the travel and investigation time of the primary officer and all the involved backup officers.

15. The data would not include that for investigation of suspicious persons, nor would it include building checks. These are considered preventative patrol activities and not calls for service.

The 1988 plan was based upon workload data between July 3, 1988 and September 24, 1988. This plan became effective January 1, 1989. Since the Savannah Police Department has been awarded the Certificate of Accreditation by the National Commission of Law Enforcement Accreditation in March 1989 it must continue to evaluate its patrol deployment structure quarterly and revise it yearly.

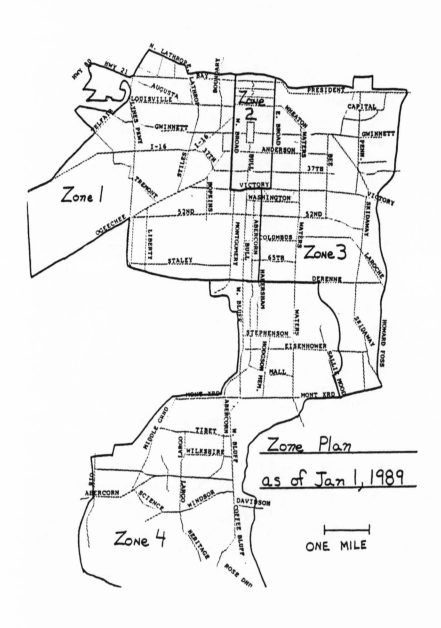

Conclusion

Since 1983 the Savannah Police Department has revised its patrol deployment allocation five times. The first study of the allocation and distribution of the patrol force was conducted by the International Association of Chiefs of Police. Based on this 1983 IACP study the patrol beats were revised based upon the current patrol strength and the weighted scores of each reported area studied. Although the IACP study influenced the Savannah Police Department of its need to revise its patrol deployment plan it was unable to prove that the police department needed an additional 48 patrol officers. However, the police force within the last four years has received additional officers. Primarily, the city could not financially afford to increase the man-power of the police department that drastically in one phase. Each year around November there has been a re-evaluation of the current beat structure. It has been necessary each year to readjust the boundaries. Savannah has the luxury of a management analyst to study the workload pattern and recommend these changes. The police managers have incorporated their knowledge of current crime patterns and predictions with these recommendations and the result has been a workable beat pattern. Although the methods were different each year, the results were satisfactory in every case except the 1986 plan of twenty beats per shift. This plan had not been based upon the calls for service data. The captains quickly found that they had very little choice as to where to deploy those officers who were not needed to fill the twenty permanent beats. The other beat plans have been accurate predictors of dispatch requirements. The crime pattern has remained in the same general area for years. This required the captains to deploy their "extra" officers to this same area every day. The result was that the officers patrolled approximately the same area as that recommended in an unused weighted average study. The drawback was that the 1986 plan required the captains to plan everyday where to deploy the "extra" officers even though they were not really extra.

Experience at Savannah Police Department has shown that the best beat structures were those that used the most recent dispatch data as a prediction of when, where, and how many officers would be needed next year. The method and formula used was less important than complete, accurate data applied with a knowledge of the geography of the city and common sense.

ENDNOTES

1. This ratio is assigned in some studies as 1.68 officers required to fill 200 beats on a yearly basis. This figure takes into consideration: regular time off, training time, annual leave holidays, sick leave, court time, military leave, accumulated overtime, AWOL, suspensions, special duty out of town, etc.

REFERENCES

Cordner, Gary W., "Police Patrol Work Load Studies: A Review and Critique", **Police Studies**, Summer 1979.

Gay, William G., **Routine Patrol Volume 1**, Washington, D.C.: U.S. Government Printing Office, 1977.

Levine, Margaret J. and Thomas McEwen. **Patrol Deployment**, Washington D.C.: National Institute of Justice, 1985.

National Advisory Commission on Criminal Justice Standards and Goals, **Task Force on Police**, Washington, D.C., 1973.

CONTRIBUTORS

Angela Kailey Gauthier received her B.A. degree in Sociology/Criminal Justice from the University of Northern Carolina. She is a correctional officer with the Colorado Department of Corrections currently working at the Colorado Womens Correctional Facility. Her duties include the personal management of inmates through both housing and security functions.

Leroy C. Gould, Ph.D. is a professor in the School of Criminology at Florida State University. His previous teaching positions include the Departments of Sociology and Psychiatry and in the Institution for Social and Policy Studies at Yale University where he was involved in research on bank robbery, motor vehicle theft, and drug treatment.

Herbert Holzman received his Ph.D. degree in Sociology at St. Johns University in Queens, New York. He is the New York State Director of the National Issues Forums Corrections Project which is one of several programs sponsored by the Kettering Foundation of Dayton, Ohio. He has five years experience teaching college courses to inmates in the New York State Prison System.

J. D. Jamieson received his M.A. and Ph.D. degrees in Criminal Justice from Sam Houston State University and holds a B.A. in Economics from the University of the South. He is currently teaching comparative justice and corrections courses in the Criminal Justice Department at Southwest Texas University. His current research interests include Latin American justice systems, substance abuse and repeat offenders, and union movements in public agencies.

Andrew Karmen, Ph.D. is an Associate Professor in the Sociology Department of John Jay College of Criminal Justice. He is the author of CRIME VICTIMS: AN INTRO-DUCTION TO VICTIMOLOGY, second edition published in 1990 by Brooks/Cole in Pacific Grove, California.

William Nardini received his B.A. degree from Cornell College of Iowa and his M.A. and Ph.D degrees in crimi-nology, sociology and law from the University of Iowa. He is a Professor at Indiana State University, Department of Criminology. Dr. Nardini is a former commissioner of correction and had been a licensed polygraph examiner for twelve years. He has written numerous articles and co-authored a textbook on law enforcement and criminal justice.

George Glenn Padgett has a B.S. degree in Chemistry from the University of Texas, Arlington. Mr. Padgett was a U.S. Army Officer from 1972-1981. He received his M.B.A. from Savannah State College in 1984. He works in the capacity of a crime analyst for the Savannah Police Depart-ment where he produces a weekly analysis of all police calls. He also conducts weekly briefings for the senior officers outlining the serious crimes for the week.

Michael J. Palmiotto received his M.A. degree from John Jay College of Criminal Justice and his Ph.D. degree from the University of Pittsburgh. He is an Associate Professor of Criminal Justice in the Department of Government, Armstrong State College, Savannah, Georgia. Dr. Palmiotto previously taught law enforcement courses at Western Illinois University and at SUNY - Brockport. He served as a police officer in New York.

Philip L. Reichel received his B.S. degree in sociology from Nebraska, Wesleyan University and both his M.A. and Ph.D.

degrees in sociology from Kansas State University, Manhattan, Kansas. He is an Associate Professor of Sociology as well as the Director of Criminal Justice studies for the Department of Sociology at the University of Northern Colorado. His articles include "The New York Times' Coverage of Executions," in a forthcoming edition of the **Journal of Contemporary Criminal Justice**, "Student Views of Crime and Criminal Justice in Poland and the United States," in a forthcoming edition of the International **Journal of Comparative and Applied Criminal Justice**, and "Southern Slave Patrols as a Transitional Police Type" in the **American Journal** of **Law and Deviance.**

Susan L. Sayles is a doctoral candidate at Florida State University in the School of Criminology. She recently completed coordinating the Attorney General's Task Force on Crimes and the Elderly in the State of Florida. Her interests include the victim's rights movement, rape and resistance, fear of crime, and crimes against the elderly.

David P. Schmidt has a M.A. in Public Policy and Ph.D. in Social Ethics from the University of Chicago. He is a consultant to senior executives on ethics issues in organizational policy and business practice. From 1984 through October 1989, he directed the Trinity Center for Ethics and Corporate Policy, an outreach program of the Parish of Trinity Church at the head of Wall Street. Dr. Schmidt is a member of the editorial advisory boards of BUSINESS ETHICS and the INTERNATIONAL JOURNAL OF VALUE-BASED MANAGEMENT. He is a trustee of the employee stock ownership plan at Quantum Chemical Corporation.

Judith D. Simon is a third year law student at Washington University in St. Louis, Missouri. She has a B.A. degree in Sociology from the University of Wisconsin. Upon completion of her law degree, she will clerk for Judge Jackson on the Federal District Court in Washington, D.C. During

1986 - 1987 Ms. Simon worked for the Michigan Department of Corrections, Western Wayne Correctional Facility, Plymouth, Michigan. There she supervised prisoners, patrolled the prison perimeter, worked as a Control Center Officer and was a payroll officer. It is here where much of the research was conducted for her article.

Rita J. Simon received her Ph.D. in Sociology at the University of Chicago in 1957. She is a University Professor in the School of Public Affairs at American University in Washington, D.C. She has authored and edited twenty books. Included among them are WOMEN AND CRIME, THE AMERICAN JURY SYSTEM, THE JURY AND THE DEFENSE OF INSANITY, THE INSANITY DEFENSE: A CRITICAL ASSESSMENT OF LAW AND POLICY IN THE POST-HINCKLEY ERA (with David Aronson), and THE FEMALE EXPERIENCE (edited with Caroline Brettell). From 1978 to 1980 she served as editor of **The American Sociological Review** and from 1983 to 1986 as editor of the **Justice Quarterly.** Her current research interests include a study of Women Rabbis and Ministers, an analysis of the Goals and Objectives of the Current and Previous Women's Movement, transracial and intercountry adoption, and the use of social science data by the Appellate Courts.

Alexander B. Smith is Professor Emeritus of Sociology at the John Jay School of Criminal Justice. He received his M.A. and Ph.D. degrees from New York University, a M.A. degree from City College of New York, his LL.B. from Brooklyn Law School and his B.S.S. from City College of New York. He is presently teaching as a Visiting Professor at the C.W. Post Campus of Long Island University for the Department of Criminal Justice and Security Administration. His publications include a forthcoming 3rd edition of CRIMINAL JUSTICE - AN OVERVIEW, for West Publishing; TREATING THE CRIMINAL OFFENDER (1988) 3rd edition for Plenum Publishing; INTRODUCTION TO PROBATION AND PAROLE; CIVIL RIGHTS AND CIVIL LIBERTIES

IN AMERICA to name a few. His articles of which there are over forty include "Retired Judges: Power and Personality off the Bench," NEW YORK LAW JOURNAL, January 18, 1990; "To What Extent Should Prosecutors Intrude in the Sentencing Process," THE JUSTICE PROFESSIONAL, Fall 1989; "Should Defendants Show Remorse?" NEW YORK LAW JOURNAL, August 25, 1989; "Exchange: The Case Against Using Biological Indicators in Judicial Decision Making," CRIMINAL JUSTICE ETHICS, (Winter-Spring 1988).

Barry D. Smith received his B.S. from Pennsylvania State University, his M.S. from Eastern Kentucky University and his Ph.D. from Sam Houston State University. He is currently an Associate Professor of Criminal Justice at Southwest Texas State University. His research interests include public sector (especially criminal justice agency) unionization.

B. Grant Stitt received his Ph.D. from the University of Arizona. He is an Associate Professor of Criminal Justice at the University of Nevada, Reno. He is interested in and has published on ethics and moral issues as they relate to victimless crimes, entrapment, the insanity defense, and the nature of evil. His articles have appeared in CRIMINOLOGY, LAW AND PHILOSOPHY, THE JOURNAL OF CRIME AND JUSTICE, CRIMINAL JUSTICE REVIEW and THE JOURNAL OF PSYCHOLOGY AND CHRISTIANITY.

Joseph L. Victor earned his B.A. and M.A. at Seton Hall University and his Doctorate of Education at Fairleigh Dickinson University. He is a professor and chairman of the Department of Law, Criminal Justice and Safety Administration at Mercy College. He serves as a coordinator of the Criminal Justice Graduate Study Program at the Westchester Campus of Long Isla:.d University. He has extensive field experience in criminal justice agencies, counseling, and administering of human service programs.

Michael Welch earned his doctorate in sociology at the University of North Texas, Denton. He is an Assistant Professor in the Department of Sociology and Anthropology at St. John's University in Queens, New York. His area of expertise includes experience in correctional institutions at the county, state and federal levels.

ABOUT THE AUTHOR

Roslyn Muraskin is a graduate of Queens College (B.A.), of New York University (M.A.) and has a Ph.D. from The City University of New York. She holds the rank of Associate Professor of Criminal Justice at the C. W. Post Campus of Long Island University and serves as the Assistant Dean for the Faculties of Accountancy, Business, Criminal Justice and Public Administration. She was associated with the Manhattan Bail Project for the Vera Institute of Justice as its Assistant Supervisor and was Supervisor of the Release on Recognizance Project for the Department of Probation, City of New York. She has developed an Instrument that measures Disparate Treatment in Correctional Facilities. She has served as editor of **The Justice Professional** and is the author of articles on "Police Work and Juveniles," in a work on **Juvenile Justice, Policies, Programs, and Services** and "Directions For The Future," in **Ethics in Criminal Justice.** She is the editor of various publications including, **Women: Victims of Domestic Violence, Rape and Criminal Justice; Criminal Justice Education: Looking Toward The Twenty-First Century;** and **Ethics In Criminal Justice.** She is a member of the Women's Division of the American Society of Criminology, and will serve on the Program Committee for the Academy of Criminal Justice Science Program Committee, 1990-1991. She is currently writing a text on WOMEN'S ISSUES IN CRIMINAL JUSTICE.